Foreword

My dear readers,

the influence of 2024 will clearly be a little more ͔
Technological development, and artificial intellige
reached a level that we believed just a few years a͵
visions that I have described in my books, I saw technologies that no one would believe existed
or would ever exist: Hospitals and medical practices without nurses and doctors, and
biotechnology and biogenetics that will make traditional agricultural plants and farmers
unnecessary … Even animal ranchers will no longer be needed, as any kind of meat will also be
artificially produced simply by pressing a button. Is all of this healthy for people? What do the
doctors, farmers, animal breeder and many others do whose work will then no longer be
needed? The large companies are not worried about that. For them, the only thing that counts
is their own profit, and they will not hesitate to influence politics in their own favor and to
bring forward legislation to promote such technologies.

Veganism will also be strongly promoted, and by successively changing our eating habits, the
younger generation will step by step lose its connection to the traditional way of life. Meat will
be specifically stigmatized as bad and the elite will establish the vegan food as a fundamental
element of the new world order.

The year 2024 holds the secret danger that all governments and organizations controlling the
world market and the ruling elites know about. These will increasingly try to set in motion
inhumane changes with long-term effects. In doing so, they will do their best to trivialize these
changes or even present them as beneficial. One goal is the total destruction of the middle
class. People's own work will lose value and society will become dependent on state benefits.
It will get enough money to live and not rebel, at least until the new world order is accepted
tacitly. Then there will be only rich and poor people.

2024 will show more and more clearly in which direction the faster technological development
is going: Humans will no longer be in first place, will be degraded and will no longer be needed
in more and more areas. It is obvious and yet does not want to be seen that technological
development brings with it many more problems: As more technology is used in industry and
in our everyday lives, more raw materials are needed, such as the water and rare earths metals
necessary for the production of computer chips. Water is essential to life, both for human
survival in general and for agriculture in particular. However, not only freshwater reserves,
but also seawater will play an increasingly important role in the global game. The technology
producing countries will suddenly become protagonists of the entire "movie." Did you know
that about 50 percent of the chips built into cell phones and computers are made in Taiwan,
the small country that once broke away from the great Republic of China?

The second largest chip-producing country is China … And now we understand China's
ambitions to annex Taiwan, don't we? Then China would control almost 90 percent of global
chip production. Now it becomes clear why suddenly there is so much conflict between the
countries of our planet. Perhaps now you begin to understand that in 2024 and in the future,
it will increasingly be about the fight for raw materials of all kinds: water controlling,

rare earths metals from Africa, technological chips from Taiwan, wheat for flour from Ukraine, corn from Latin America, oil and gas from Russia, Europe's huge energy reserves from Greece and Cyprus... But there is also explosive atmosphere about ethical and constitutional issues in America or the Chinese hegemonic strategy. Iran and Israel will not be able to find a solution for peaceful coexistence. The same can be said of Serbia and Albania about Kosovo. All these themes hold the danger of turning the present world order upside down to such an extreme that I would like to dispense with further analysis.

Humans in 2024 are increasingly playing the role of unpaid background actors. There is a great danger that everything humanity has ever achieved will be lost just because of the greed of the global elites. 2024 could be a simulation of the Second World War, or even worse. Can you imagine what happens if electric power no longer exists and we got to live without electricity for a few years? The negative aspects will continue until autumn 2026. After that, the situation will slowly relax and get better. 2029 to 2032 will then become very important years again from an astrological point of view. But let's focus on 2024, when the situation will become more acute compared to the year before. Humanity will be faced with major political and social changes on a global scale and natural disasters with enormous destructive power, and it will be more and more a matter of survival. Another aspect of 2024 wants no more religion and promotes ecumenism and only one religion accepted by all. This will stir up religious groups and mobilize protests against religious globalization.

Until August 2024, negative happenings will dominate the world and the stock market, and a large banking crisis may well be possible again. Large companies with a long tradition will have to close and there is also the danger of a shortage of goods and energy again. Further rising costs for electricity, heating, water and food will make everyday life more and more expensive and make people more and more poor.

Aphrodite and Ares were in Capricorn when the war in Ukraine started in February 2022. Two years later, in February 2024, Aphrodite and Ares find themselves together again, this time in Aquarius. This constellation could bring about an end to the war, or at least a very significant happening in this conflict. However, Pluto in Aquarius creates global trouble and will continue until the end of 2026.

2024 further brings our attention to refugees and all people leaving their country to look for protection and a new chance of luck. People from other religions and cultures will try in masses to escape to a safe country – legal or illegal. Opposite them, there will be many disillusioned people who want to travel back to their home countries. There will be terrible conflicts between these two movements of people, although 2024 also offers an opportunity for understanding and acceptance.

2024 also prepares the end of dictatorships and totalitarian regimes! Possibly even the beginning of the dissolution of the European dream. One of the strongest country of Europe will be the reason of a possible European divorce. The war in Ukraine and the danger that the Russian federation demand all old USSR Territories back because of the violation of the Warsaw Pact will bring nightmares to many European countries, especially to Germany. 2024 is a year, which brings many changes on global level and the parting from so far valid rules and values.

From a spiritual point of view, many unseen evil deities and very dangerous energies are free everywhere all around the world causing violent acts, catastrophes and chaos. It is very important for every lightworker to put an extra effort trying to support harmony and sending healing good vibes everywhere. The frequencies of the earth and the universe will be reset, global warming turns to be the new Ice Age. Extreme heating is a reaction of our planet and maybe its getting colder and not warmer! This entails important happenings for our world as well as for the entire solar system. 2024 will be a very important year for all those who connect with the Higher Power, as it offers a favorable "net" that promotes praying and wishing.

Stay healthy and mindful! I hope you enjoy the Witchbook 2024 with a fully Calendar, Witch Knowledge, Lunar Dates and Astrology!

With light and love,
Nik W. D. Goodman

Content

Witch calendar with moon phases for each day, planetary days, info about the witch festivals as well as goddesses and gods, monthly tendencies and **large yearly horoscope for all zodiac signs**   6 – 150

Witchcraft knowledge:

Celtic tree horoscope	7
The Gregorian calendar	11
Planet hours and how to calculate them	13
Witch symbol: Pentagram	17
2024: Chinese Year of the Dragon / Chinese Horoscope	22 – 26
Prayer to Hecate / Witch symbol: Hecate's wheel"	28
Witch symbol: Triskele	30
Suitable tools for magical processes	35
Divination arts: Tasseography, Ceromancy and Molybdomancy, Ovomancy	37 – 39
Egg oracle ritual at Ostara or on the day of the Easter moon	42 – 43
Use the power of the moon: The full moon and the new moon	47
Witch symbols: Celtic Knot and All-Seeing Eye	49
Witch symbol: Spiral Goddess	55
The 7 Knots Love Ritual	58 – 59
Witch symbol: Triangle	61 – 62
Use the power of the moon: The waxing moon	64
Witch symbol: Circle	66
Use the power of the moon: The waning moon	66
Witch symbols: Horned God and Triple Moon	72
Dragon oil and Dragon powder recipe	75
Runes: The Ancient Futhark	79 – 82
Witch symbol: Hexagram	84
Sokushinbutsu: Mummified monks	86
Witch symbol: Anch	88
Magic plants	90
Witch symbol: Cross	96
The candle flame and what it shows us	96
Harvesting medicinal plants according to the moon	98

Oil extract from flowers and herbs	98
Chakras: Their central themes and ways to happiness	100
Lucid dreaming	104 – 106
Properties and effects of the moon phases in relation to health and medicines	108
Aphrodite and Selene: what suits them	110
Helios and Zeus: what suits them	112
The 12 houses in astrology and the horoscope	114
Witch broom ritual to get rid of unwanted guests	118
Prayer to Demeter	120
Greek deities	122
The magic of trees	129
Hermes and what suits him	131
The very special meaning of the trees for the Celts	133
Ares and what suits him	137
Properly cleanse and consecrate ritual objects / Ritual magic mirror	140
Cronos and what suits him	142
Our Aura: Visible energy of the soul / Why is it important to cleanse your aura?	144
The magic of the "Rauh" Nights	145 – 146
"Rauh" Night Ritual to manifest a wish	146 – 147
Artavan, the unknown fourth Holy King	148
Miracles around the icon of the Blessed Virgin Mary in the Holy Mount Athos	149 – 150

Witch info compact:

Moon Calendar 2024	151
Yearly overview with witch festivals, moon phases, eclipses and zodiac signs	152
Spiritually positive and negative days	153
Magic processes and planets	153
The phases of the moon and the matching gardening	154

January

CW 1	♑	***Capricorn** 22.12. – 19.01.* *🌿 Fir – Tree of foresight: 02. - 11.01.*
Mon 1	☾ 🌘	Feast of the goddess Nanshe **New Year's Day**, Solemnity of Mother Mary
Tue 2	♂ 🌘	
Wed 3 +	☿ 🌘	St. Genoveva
Thu 4	♃ 🌗	half moon waning
Fri 5	♀ 🌘	
Sat 6	♄ 🌘	Three Kings Day / Dia de los Reyes ✝ *Christmas (+ 07.01.), Theophany, Baptism of Jesus Christ,* 💎 *King's Day celebration in honor of the new tribal officers & Antelope, Buffalo and Deer Dances*
Sun 7	☉ 🌘	✝ *Synaxis of Johannes (Forerunner and Baptist)*

*+ spiritually positive days **-** spiritually negative days*
*Celebration / Commemoration: ✝ Orthodox - **I** Islamic - **J** Jewish - **H** Hindu -*
***B** Buddhist - 💎 American Indian*

Monthly trend January	love	friends, family	profession, money
Aries	☼☼☼	☼☼☼☼☼	☼
Taurus	☼☼☼☼☼	☼☼☼☼	☼☼
Gemini	☼☼☼☼☼	☼☼☼☼	☼☼☼
Cancer	☼☼☼	☼☼☼	☼☼☼☼☼
Leo	☼☼	☼☼☼☼☼	☼☼☼☼☼
Virgo	☼☼☼	☼☼☼	☼☼☼☼
Libra	☼☼☼	☼☼☼☼☼	☼☼☼☼
Scorpio	☼☼☼☼☼	☼☼☼☼	☼☼
Sagittarius	☼☼☼☼	☼☼☼	☼☼☼☼☼
Capricorn	☼☼☼☼☼	☼☼☼☼☼	☼☼☼☼
Aquarius	☼☼	☼☼☼☼☼	☼☼☼☼
Pisces	☼☼☼☼☼	☼☼	☼☼☼☼☼

Goddess Nanshe

The Babylonian-Sumerian water goddess is a goddess of fertility, "Bright Seeing" and "True Saying" as well as dreams and dream interpretation. She sees the omens for the coming year and on New Year's Day she also reviews the past year and judges people's deeds. So this day is perfect for asking cards about the future in her name, for example.

Celtic tree horoscope
The personal tree of life in the Celtic tree circle

The Celtic tree circle is an entrance to the universal knowledge of the ancient peoples. It gives an insight into the fascinating world of trees and their magical powers. The Celts were connected with nature to a much greater extent than we humans are today. They lived in complete harmony with their environment, animals and plants. Especially the trees played a very important role for the Celts in the field of mysticism and so they gave special qualities and characters to every kind of tree. These characteristics are reflected in the Celtic tree horoscope. Depending on the date of birth in the Celtic year cycle, the tree horoscope assigns a tree of life to each person, which can tell a lot about their personality. **There are a total of 21 trees of life in the Celtic tree circle. The four main trees - oak, birch, olive tree, beech - take up one day each.** The other 17 trees divide the year into 35 sections of different lengths. 16 trees appear twice and are opposite each other in the year circle - once on the light and once on the dark side of the year. The poplar (tree of self-knowledge) even appears three times.

When which tree of life has its time is noted in the head of the calendar.

Capricorn 22.12. – 19.01.

Capricorn is ambitious, aspiring, progressive, politically interested and has a strong sense of humor. Negative characteristics of this zodiac sign are the tendency to complain, feel oppressed and worry, pessimism, miserliness and callousness.

Good time for magical work, dealing with issues ambition, career, recognition and organization busy

Planet: Cronos (Saturn) / **Angel:** Cassiel / **Olympian spirit:** Aratron / **Element:** earth / **Lucky stones:** amber, onyx, sapphire, quartz / **Colors:** earthy tones, yellow, blue, black, green / **Lucky day:** Saturday / **Metal:** lead / **Animals:** crocodile, seahorse, robin / **Body parts influenced:** teeth, bones, joints, skin

Capricorn in 2024

2024 promises you that you can be successful at work and take a step forward in your career if you are willing to work hard and with a positive attitude. Maintaining social contacts is also important for getting ahead. A strenuous time awaits you, which often dampens your optimism. But take comfort in the fact that the most difficult time is already behind you. The whereabouts of Kronos (Saturn) in the zodiac sign of Pisces in 2024 will help you find new allies, sources of energy and solutions to financial problems, as well as make necessary purchases that have been long delayed. At the beginning of the year you will experience a busy time, which will cause a lot of stress, but will also bring you quite a bit further professionally. Between 01. January and 20. February, you are mentally very strong and courageous, preparing the ground for improving your circumstances. It is a favorable time for renting or selling real estate, and joyful events around your home and family (a move or the arrival of a new family member for example) further strengthen you. Starting in early spring, make concrete decisions about your future path in life. Build a solid foundation for your future and stop wasting time on unnecessary things. Concentrate on what is really important to you and start to realize it. Important here is a thoughtful and not impulsive approach. New acquaintances as well as made agreements and wise decisions have a long-term and very positive perspective for your future.

During the year you will be confronted with significant changes and it is necessary to accept them so that your current situation improves. Be open to the new that comes into your life and don't be afraid to approach things differently than before. A fresh perspective will give you the opportunity to learn new things and put those new skills to beneficial use. You are about to finally close important chapters of your life and leave them behind to be ready for new ways.

The year 2024 brings important restructuring in terms of home, family and work and you will take some solid steps forward. Especially the months of the two solar eclipses, April and October, are particularly critical times with radical changes here. It is even possible that you will break up with your partner. March and April will bring significant gains, so you should focus strongly on the financial sector during this time. After insecurities and jealousy in love will trouble you from March, you can look forward to a happy and intense love life in the period from May to July, and also in the last two months of the year. July and September are two important months to make commitments that will bring you closer to your success and significantly reduce your financial worries.

This year you will accomplish a lot by taking risks and actively taking charge of your life. Come out of your shell and start making your plans a reality. Great projects will come into your life if you put your skills to proper use. A positive attitude and optimism will enable you to achieve the highest level of success.

Capricorn: love, family and friends

2024 will help you cultivate a favorable climate in your relationships. Give everything to bring fresh wind into your partnership and fight boredom and monotony. It is very important that you do not let third parties influence you in terms of partnership. Draw clear boundaries to keep jealous people at bay. You will make few new acquaintances in 2024 and some of your old friends will no longer accompany you on your life's journey with its drastic changes. The planets align in your favor. The year 2024, with its special planetary constellations, also gives you a lot of creativity and empathy to breathe new life into old acquaintances that have broken up over the years, mostly through your fault. Listen to your heart and less to your mind. Be open to the people who will enter your life anew in 2024 and get involved with them. This is especially true for the singles among the Capricorns. Open your heart and give love a chance! The lunar eclipses in March as well as in September and October warn you against arrogance, jealousy and greed in love.

On a family level, cultivate memories with your loved ones that strengthen family bonds and find ways to resolve differences that have arisen between you before things get out of hand. Show your family that they can count on you. This year you will have a strong need to make others happy. However, be careful not to put your desires completely on the back burner for the sake of your family and your partner. You need to find a good balance here.

Capricorn: profession and finances

You will also have many successes on a professional level, especially at the beginning of 2024. You will be able to express your thoughts and ideas without any problems and they will be heard and taken seriously. It is important that you define your goals with care and consideration and only pursue those plans where you can count on support. After all, it is almost impossible for you to make it on your own. Above all, orient yourself to the ideas that will open up new opportunities for you and with which you can develop professionally, but also in the area of social skills. Your financial stability will allow you to take care of your needs, fulfill your desires and also pay off debts. There are also good prospects of unexpected windfalls, for example through an inheritance. Nevertheless, you should be careful not to spend too much in order to maintain your truly healthy financial position in the long term.

Capricorn: health

For most of the year, you will enjoy good health. However, there are a few things you need to do to stay healthy: make sure you eat right, get enough sleep and exercise. If you do get surprised by symptoms of illness, take them seriously and rather get medical advice and help once too often.

January

CW 2	♑	**Capricorn** *22.12. - 19.01.*
		🌿 *Elm – Tree of awakening: 12. – 24.01.*
Mon 8	☽	
Tue 9	♂	St. Gregor
Wed 10 +	☿	St. Paulus
Thu 11	♃ / ☉	new moon
Fri 12 -	♀ / ☾	† Αλώα †
Sat 13	♃ / ☾	
Sun 14	☉ / ☾	† New Year – Gregorian Calendar

~ 10 ~

The Gregorian calendar

The Gregorian calendar, which is based on the course of the sun, became established worldwide, even though some cultures have other calendar systems. The ancient Greek calendar system is the oldest, basing its calculations on the moon. The Hellenics, as well as the Babylonians and also the Chinese, used a calendar in which the months of the calendar corresponded to the natural lunar months. Since each lunar month lasts 29.5 days, the Athenians added an embolic 13th month every 3 years to keep the months in line with the seasons.

Back to the origin of the Gregorian calendar, which is based on the Julian calendar: in 46 BC, during the reign of Julius Caesar, the year was fixed at 365.25 days (365 days and six 6 hours): an attempt to mathematically approximate the 365.2422 Earth rotations of a solar year. However, the so-called Julian year is 11 minutes and 14 seconds too long compared to the solar year, so that the deviation already amounted to more than seven days in the 14th century.

For this reason, Pope Gregory XIII reformed the calendar system in 1582. To balance out the difference to the solar year, ten days were simply skipped in October 1582 and then counted on. In addition, switching rules were to work against the differences in the future. At about the same time, the beginning of the year also changed. This was still in the Middle Ages at different times. But now the 01. January was officially fixed as the beginning of the new year. Probably this choice has to do with the winter solstice as well as the birth of Jesus Christ. Much of the world gradually adopted this calendar, most recently by China in 1949, but the Orthodox Church did not go along with this reform. Orthodox translates as "straight" and so it stuck to its line, which is why many Orthodox Christians still celebrate Christmas on 06. and 07. January.

$$\Omega \diamondsuit \Omega$$

*If you're hiding the truth,
even though you know them,
it's like this,
as if you were burying gold.*
Pythagoras

January

CW 3	≈≈	***Aquarius*** *20.01 – 18.02.* (previously Capricorn)
Mon 15	☾)	**H** *Makar Sankranti - Pongal (until 18.01.)*
Tue 16	♂)	St. Marcellus
Wed 17	☿)	World Day of Religions, Blessing of the Animals, St. Antonius
Thu 18	♃ ◐	**half moon waxing** Martin Luther King Day
Fri 19	♀ ●	
Sat 20	♄ ●	✝ *Timkat Festival (Ethiopian Orthodox)*　　**Aquarius** > 18.02. St. Fabian, St. Sebastian
Sun 21	☉ ●	St. Agnes, St. Vincent

~ 12 ~

Planet hours and how to calculate them

All following hours result according to an order which arranges the planets from a geocentric perspective according to their increasing speed:

1. **Cronos** (Saturn), 2. **Zeus** (Jupiter), 3. **Ares** (Mars), 4. **Helios** (Sun),
5. **Aphrodite** (Venus), 6. **Hermes** (Mercury), 7. **Selene** (Moon)

To calculate the planetary hours correctly, you need to **divide** the **time span of the day** (from sunrise to sunset) **into 12 parts**. For example, if the day begins at 6 am and ends at 8 pm, then you have 14 hours or 840 minutes. These divide You divide by 12 and get 70 minutes per planetary hour for that day. You apply the same procedure for the hours of the night. For example, if this starts at 8 pm and ends at 6 am, then you have 10 nighttime hours, or 600 minutes, which you divide by 12 again. So in this case the planetary night hours are 50 minutes long. So you see: **Only very rarely the planetary hours correspond to the normal time hours with 60 minutes.**

Each day begins with a different planetary time

The first hour after sunrise is fixed for each day. Monday, for example, begins with the planetary time of Selene (Moon), because Monday is "ruled" by her. Tuesday begins with the planetary time of Ares (Mars) ... If you look at the Latin origin of the weekday names, this connection to the planets becomes clearly visible:

            Monday - *Dies Lunae* - *Moon, Luna (Selene)*
             Tuesday - *Dies Martis* - *Mars (Ares)*
           Wednesday - *Dies Mercuri* - *Mercury (Hermes)*
             Thursday - *Dies Jovis* - *Jupiter (Zeus)*
              Friday - *Dies Veneris* - *Venus (Aphrodite)*
             Saturday - *Dies Saturni* - *Saturn (Cronos)*
              Sunday - *Dies Solis* - *Sun (Helios)*

A calculation example

Sunday / sunrise 6:00 and sunset 20:00 /
70 minutes per planetary hour during the day and 50 minutes per planetary hour at night

Planetary hours of the day: 06.00: Helios, 07.10: Aphrodite, 08.20: Hermes, 9.30: Selene, 10.40: Cronos, 11.50: Zeus, 13.00: Ares, 14.10: Helios, 15.20: Aphrodite, 16.30: Hermes, 17.40: Selene, 18.50: Cronos, 19.00: Zeus

Planetary hours of the night: 20.10: Ares, 21.00: Helios, 21.50: Aphrodite, 22.40: Hermes, 23.30: Selene, 00.20: Cronos, 01.10: Zeus, 02.00: Ares, 02.50: Helios, 03.40: Aphrodite, 04.30: Hermes, 05.20: Selene

Aquarius 20.01. – 18.02.

Aquarians are helpful, have a progressive outlook on life, usually also artistic or scientific talents. The unpredictable Aquarius often falls in love, tends to exaggerated romanticism.

Good time for magic work on the aspects freedom, creative expression, psychic abilities, friendship, science and letting go of bad habits

Planets: Cronos (Saturn) and Uranus / **Angel:** Cassiel / **Olympian spirit:** Aratron / **Element:** air / **Lucky stones:** amber, onyx, zircon / **Colors:** green, blue, ice blue, metallic colors / **Lucky day:** Saturday / **Lucky numbers:** 9, 39, 49 / **Flowers:** azalea, poppy, lily of the valley, carnation / **Metal:** lead / **Animals:** raven, kangaroo, zebra, giraffe, greyhound / **Body parts influenced:** calves, ankles, varicose veins, circulatory system

Aquarius in 2024

2024 will be full of hope, optimism, enthusiasm and positive developments for you. Plans that have long been abandoned suddenly take on concrete form. Let the people around you inspire and motivate you and remember that it is never too late to work on realizing your dreams. There are some new opportunities coming up and it is up to you to boldly take advantage of them. However, especially in the spring months, you will be plagued by doubts as to whether the path you have chosen is the right one. You will notice that the realization of your wishes will put your nerves to a hard test at first. But you will find a way to fight your fears and uncertainties. Push all inhibiting thoughts aside. Besides, you are not alone. You have people by your side who care about you and on whom you can rely.

In 2024 you will gain many valuable insights about yourself, your partnership and also the relationships with your fellow human beings. This will let you face life with more self-confidence and help you to master challenges. Your increasing dissatisfaction in the past two years is the motor for you in 2024 to finally change something: In the professional as well as in the interpersonal area you bring a breath of fresh air into your everyday life with creative ideas and newly made experiences. Thus, you also close the painful gaps that have arisen in your life since 2019 due to quarrels, losses and separations. Business trips will bring additional variety. However, the changes also bring greater responsibility and you need to be well organized to successfully manage your new life. It is also very important that you not only turn to the professional sphere, but also bring the new momentum into your private life. Otherwise, there is a risk of changes that you do not want.

In some moments of 2024 you will be confronted with yourself: with your hidden and secret side, your negative instincts, your passions and weaknesses. Your thirst for distinction, conquest and achieving your goals regardless is definitely a threat to be taken seriously.

Aquarius: love, family and friends

Aphrodite, as the planet of love, has planned for 2024 to exert her full influence so that you can have a healthy and happy partnership, possibly consolidated by marriage followed by starting a family. Moments full of passion and romance, perhaps a confession of love, await you in 2024. Deep desires around love will become reality!

It will be easy for you to express your feelings to your partner. Your partnership is characterized by good communication and a lot of understanding for the other. Also for those among Aquarians who have had a breakup and are currently alone, 2024 is a good year to start a new relationship. However, it is important to overcome self-pity in order to be open for the new partner.

As for family matters, you will not know what to do first. There are many "construction sites" that need to be taken care of. But in order for everything to run harmoniously, you should first deal with yourself and only then create order in the domestic sphere and / or take responsibility for other family members. And don't be afraid to take responsibility for them the other way around, too.

2024 is a favorable year for Aquarians to expand their social contacts and also expand your knowledge through the diversity of your new acquaintances. Be open and do not isolate yourself. Friends from the past as well as old loves will return to your life. You are definitely one of the winners in 2024 as far as love is concerned.

Aquarius: profession and finances

Your career will be on the upswing in 2024. Your colleagues and superiors will be proud of you and there is a good chance of a salary increase or promotion. It is important that you are adaptable and able to compromise. Then you will manage to realize your professional desires and obtain privileges. Especially in the times around the eclipses, be careful and very prudent in your professional tasks, as mistakes will then have personal consequences. If possible, you should avoid a professional reorientation in 2024. Take your time and first examine your options in your current field of work. Stick to what you are doing until the time is ripe for professional change.

At the beginning of 2024, it is advisable to organize your finances well, get an overview of them and handle your money carefully. Then, from mid-May, your financial situation will improve radically, so you will even have surplus money to save and invest in new projects. However, you should avoid impulse buying, especially if you can't manage your finances properly.

Aquarius: health

Aquarians must take great care of their health in 2024 and strengthen their immune system in every way possible. Keep fit by eating healthy and exercising daily. Especially if you suffer from chronic health problems, you must be very careful in 2024 and rather go to the doctor once too much than once too little.

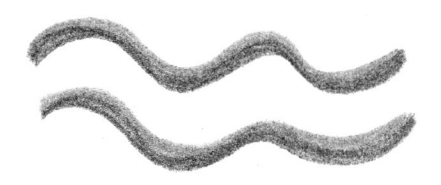

January

CW 4	♒	**_Aquarius_** 20.01. - 18.02.
		🌿 **_Cypress – Tree of eternity:_** _25.01. – 03.02._
Mon 22	☽ ●	
Tue 23 -	♂ ●	💎 _San Ildefonso feast day_
Wed 24	☿ ●	**J** _Tu biShevat (+ 25.01.)_, International Day of Education
Thu 25	♃ ○	**full moon: Wolf Moon,** ✝ _Conversion of St. Paul_
Fri 26	♀ ●	St. Timotheus † _Λήναια_ †
Sat 27 +	♄ ●	International Day in Memory of the Victims of the Holocaust
Sun 28	☉ ●	

January Full Moon
Wolf Moon

The Native American Indigenous refer to the moon in January as the "Wolf Moon." This naming was inspired by the hungry wolves that howl outside settlements in winter.

Witch symbol: Pentagram

The pentagram is a very strong symbol of protection. Its main function is to protect against evil. In Goethe's famous work "Faust", the devil Mephistopheles cannot leave Faust's room after his first visit. This is because there is a stone pentagram above the door. So it is the definitive protection symbol and belongs to our main arsenal! The pentagram is a powerful protective tool in exorcism.

The two horizontal and the two downward pointing tips symbolize the four elements fire, water, air and earth. The fifth, pointing upwards, symbolizes the spirit and the divine. The pentagram encourages to see life as a whole and as a cycle. It symbolizes birth, baptism (initiation), love, rest and death. And also the five natural senses: sight, hearing, touch, smell and taste. The number 5 also represents the male and female universe and the sum of the father (3) and the Mother (2).

Devilish pentagram

If the tip of the 5-pointed star points downwards, then it is a symbol used in black magic art and Satanism. The two points of the star pointing upwards symbolize the two horns of Satan. Overall, the upside down star shows a man hanging upside down with his legs open. The reversal of the pentagram attests the reversal of human nature and so expresses the abhorrence of the divine word.

January / February

CW 5	♒	**Aquarius** 20.01. – 18.02.
		🌿 *Poplar – Tree of self-knowledge:* 04. – 08.02.
Mon 29	☾ ●	
Tue 30	♂ ●	*Jazhn-e Sadeh - Sadeh Festival (Iran / Persia)*
Wed 31 +	☿ ●	
Thu 1	♃ ●	Feast of the oddess Juno Februata
Fri 2 -	♀ ●	**Imbolc**, Candlemas, midwinter, Presentation of the Lord 💎 *Candelaria Festival (Picuris Pueblo)*
Sat 3	♄ ◐	**half moon waning** *Setsubun sai festival (Japan)*
Sun 4	☉ ☽	

~ 18 ~

Monthly trend February	love	friends, family	profession, money
Aries	☼☼☼☼☼	☼☼☼☼☼	☼☼☼
Taurus	☼☼☼☼☼	☼☼☼	☼☼☼
Gemini	☼☼☼	☼☼☼☼☼	☼
Cancer	☼☼☼☼☼	☼☼☼☼	☼☼☼
Leo	☼	☼	☼☼☼
Virgo	☼☼☼	☼☼☼☼☼	☼☼☼
Libra	☼☼☼☼	☼☼☼☼	☼☼☼☼☼
Scorpio	☼☼	☼☼	☼☼
Sagittarius	☼☼☼☼☼	☼	☼☼☼☼☼
Capricorn	☼☼☼☼	☼☼	☼☼
Aquarius	☼☼	☼☼☼☼☼	☼☼
Pisces	☼☼☼	☼☼	☼☼☼☼☼

Goddess Juno Februata

Wolf Power

In the night to the 01. February is the festival in honor of the goddess Juno Februata. She is the Roman patroness and goddess of love passion and erotic love. She is the virgin mother of the god Ares (Mars), whom she conceived from a lily. Women offered flowers as sacrifices to the goddess and their husbands, representing the goddess, gave them flowers. People celebrated a pleasurable, erotic festival of the female wolf (the goddess Acca Larentia suckled the twins Romulus and Remus in the form of a wolf), also called Lupercalia.

Imbolc / Candlemas   *2. February*

Imbolc is the festival in honor of the fire goddess Brigit or Bride, daughter of Dagda and second patron saint of Ireland. It is the festival of light. After Imbolc, the goddess Moon has begun to recover from the birth of God (God Sun). God Sun is a small and lively boy who grows bigger every day, warming up the earth with his growing power and making vegetation blossom. Imbolc is a celebration of purification after the dark period of winter. In the past, it was the custom in many European countries to light large fires in the center of villages to bring warmth and light even before spring. Candle flames were also supposed to drive away the dark days. That is why this festival was also called Candlemas.

Imbolc is considered an ideal day to accept new members into a coven, a coven of witches. On Imbolc witches lit candles and lamps all over the house after sunset and honored God the Sun, who will now bring more light and warmth from day to day. Imbolc's colors are white and orange. On the altar there is a wheel to symbolize the cycle of the year, and it is decorated with flowers (for example, heather or snowdrops). Incense: innamon, myrrh and rosemary.

February

CW 6	♒	**_Aquarius_** *20.01. - 18.02.*
		Cedar – Tree of mystery: 09. – 18.02.
Mon 5	☽	St. Agatha
Tue 6	♂	*I Isra and Mi'raj (+ 07.02.)*, St. Dorothea
Wed 7 +	☿	
Thu 8 +	♃	Carnival starts (Dirty Thursday)
Fri 9	♀ ☉	**new moon**, *Chinese New Year*, St. Appolonia
Sat 10 -	♄	*I Start Ramadan (until 09.04.)*, **B** *Losar*
Sun 11	☉	International Day of Women and Girls in Science

Chinese Year of the Dragon 10.02.2024 – 28.01.2025

The Chinese New Year is celebrated according to ancient tradition approximately in the period between January and February at new moon. The cycle of sixty years on which this lunar calendar is based is composed of the five main elements: metal, water, wood, fire and earth.

The twelve animals that shape these cycles dominate the Chinese Zodiac for one lunar year at a time. According to legend, Buddha called the animals to him one day to say goodbye, but only twelve came: first the rat, then the buffalo, tiger, rabbit, dragon, snake, horse, goat, monkey, rooster, dog and finally the pig. Buddha had given each animal a year on which it was allowed to put its stamp. This is how the twelve-year rhythm in Chinese astrology came about.

龙

In 2024, the dragon "reigns". He is a winning type and blessed with luck, wealth and power. He has enormous strength and is very self-confident. He has high demands on himself and others and needs a lot of recognition.

Candle art: Magic guardian dragons by SPIRITUAL ART

Chinese Horoscope

Year of the Dragon ~ 1940, 1952, 1964, 1976, 1988, 2000, 2012, 2024

A winner / blessed with luck, wealth and power
Strengths: versatile, confident, dynamic, powerful, passionate
Weaknesses: ruthless, opinionated, arrogant

The dragon is very imposing, extremely active and determined. He has enormous power. Blessed with luck, wealth and power, he encounters life generously and powerfully. As a doer, he often makes it to leadership positions and he needs a challenging task. He is considered to be very talented, intelligent, enthusiastic and kind and passionate. He has high standards. Thanks to his healthy self-confidence, he is aware of his greatness and needs a lot of recognition.

Year of the Snake ~ 1941, 1953, 1965, 1977, 1989, 2001, 2013, 2025

A wise judge of character / enigmatic, clever and charismatic
Strengths: smart, deep, intuitive, peace-loving
Weaknesses: moody, jealous, manipulative

The reserved and refined snake is a deep thinker. She is a good observer with patience and feeling for the right time to play the trump card up her sleeve. A snake has a lot of intuition for others, but reveals little of herself and does not immediately trust everyone. She is peace-loving and can also be manipulative. Her cleverness, sharp mind and 7th sense ensure that her standard of living is always up to par. Her organizational skills make her successful.

Year of the Horse ~ 1942, 1954, 1966, 1978, 1990, 2002, 2014, 2026

A restless entertainer / fun-loving, freedom-loving and optimistic
Strengths: dynamic, flexible, open, sociable, fun-loving
Weaknesses: unrestrained, erratic, restless, selfish

The horse is bursting with vitality. It is extroverted, witty, bright, adventurous, spirited and loves its freedom. Its cheerful and talkative nature makes it very popular. It is imaginative and has linguistic talent. Its impulsive and dynamic nature needs a lot of exercise to stay balanced and healthy. The horse is flexible and enthusiastic. Its sure instinct leads it to the goal and it does not lose its optimism even if something does not work out.

Year of the Goat ~ 1943, 1955, 1967, 1979, 1991, 2003, 2015, 2027

A good soul / carefree, warm-hearted benefactor
Strengths: compassionate, understanding, caring, helpful, creative
Weaknesses: stifling, dependent, spoiled, melancholic, jealous

The goat is subtle, imaginative, warm-hearted, trusting, reserved and very affectionate. She loves peace and harmony very much and it is difficult to start an argument with her. She is very compassionate and always has an open ear for the sorrow of those around her. She can't always deal with her own feelings as calmly as it may seem on the outside.

Due to her rich emotional world, she is very mood-dependent, but also very creative. A little more stability would be helpful for her in everyday life. She has a hard time with organization and discipline.

Year of the Monkey ~ 1944, 1956, 1968, 1980, 1992, 2004, 2016, 2028

A cheerful genius / solve any problem with panache
Strengths: imaginative, flexible, optimistic, mentally very agile, cheerful
Weaknesses: unscrupulous, haughty, envious, unable to take criticism

The monkey has an ingenious resourcefulness and great talent for improvisation. Nothing is impossible for him. Mentally and physically he seeks the challenge and is always in motion. He is a cheerful and popular companion, loves parties and inspires with sparkling wit. With his inventive spirit and flexible organizational talent, he manages everything seemingly with his left hand. Sometimes the monkey feels superior to others because of this. He is enthusiastic about everything new, but sometimes he doesn't have the necessary time and concentration for it. Criticism is hard for him to tolerate.

Year of the Rooster ~ 1945, 1957, 1969, 1981, 1993, 2005, 2017, 2029

A shimmering perfectionist / with devotion to completeness
Strengths: worldly, perfectionist, upright, down-to-earth, hard-working, helpful
Weaknesses: sensitive to criticism, immoderate

The rooster is an extravagant, style-conscious and charming entertainer. He is very perfectionist, down to earth and neat. He impresses at work with diligence, organizational skills and sincerity. Prestigious objects are very important to the rooster. He is self-confident, humorous and an eloquent speaker, which opens many doors for him, especially in love. However, he also looks for harmony and permanent exchange. With his positive, helpful nature and elegant, extravagant style, he wins many hearts.

Year of the Dog ~ 1946, 1958, 1970, 1982, 1994, 2006, 2018, 2030

A selfless hero / a heart of gold
Strengths: responsible, fair, loyal
Weaknesses: dogmatic, pessimistic, cynical

The dog has good knowledge of human nature and great empathy. He is sincere, affectionate, helpful and very reliable. His good-natured and responsible nature and clear moral values make him popular. Justice, reason and the common good are important to him and he needs security and stability. He is loyal and wants trust and security from his partner. He is pessimistic by nature and smells danger everywhere. He has a firm opinion from which he very rarely deviates.

Year of the Pig ~ 1947, 1959, 1971, 1983, 1995, 2007, 2019, 2031

A good-natured enjoyer / his happiness is legendary
Strengths: good-natured, tolerant, generous, trustworthy
Weaknesses: stubborn, comfortable, moody

The good-natured, generous, helpful and livable pig is very tolerant, cannot lie and is therefore very trustworthy. Luck is always on its side. Therefore, it is optimistic and always believes in the good in people. For the fun-loving pig there is always something to celebrate. His slogan: live and let live. It loves amusements and sociability and can enjoy quite dissolutely. It seeks harmony and avoids quarrels if possible. However, it can become quite furious if you catch it in a sore spot.

Year of the Rat ~ 1948, 1960, 1972, 1984, 1996, 2008, 2020, 2032

A smart fighter / intelligent charm with bite
Strengths: persistent, healthy egoism, generous, sociable, ambitious
Weaknesses: intriguing, careerist, dogmatic, addicted to criticism

The rat knows how to fight his way to the top with a lot of charisma. In doing so, she often doesn't act very considerately. Luck does not fall into her lap. The versatile, outgoing Rat makes friends easily. She is full of surprises and it is certainly not boring with her. She is a cheerful individualist and bon vivant with dazzling charm. Her slogan is: all or nothing. Her mind is razor sharp. If something goes wrong, she picks herself up again immediately. She doesn't like it when people interfere in her affairs.

Year of the Buffalo ~ 1949, 1961, 1973, 1985, 1997, 2009, 2021, 2033

A rock in the surf / in the calm lies the strength
Strengths: strong-willed, ambitious, straightforward, down-to-earth, loyal, reliable
Weaknesses: stubborn, unrestrained, often too cautious, intolerant

The buffalo likes a quiet life without much stress. He has no great demands, but security is extremely important to him. He does not think much of change. He prefers to rely on the tried and tested. The Buffalo is strong-willed, cautious and absolutely down-to-earth. He reaches his goal with straightforward determination, is ambitious and extremely reliable. He is practical and approaches life in a very organized way. He is the rock in the surf. The quiet loner does not let himself be fooled. Although a buffalo seems rather reserved, he likes to be in charge.

Year of the Tiger ~ 1950, 1962, 1974, 1986, 1998, 2010, 2022, 2034

A warm-hearted adventurer / the elixir of life is called self-realization
Strengths: honest, passionate, brave, tenacious
Weaknesses: reckless, fickle, selfish, imperious

With a lot of intelligence, but also ruthlessness, the tiger realizes his goals. Whoever gets in his way should watch out. He is impulsive, passionate, daring, fearless and has a fighting temperament. Where others reach their limits, it is only exciting for the tiger. The world is his stage and he perceives life as an exciting game. He loves adventure and is very emotional. For his fearless and passionate way of life, he is admired by others. For a tiger, nothing is worse than routine. He needs a lot of freedom and inspiration and his goal is absolute self-realization.

Year of the Rabbit ~ 1951, 1963, 1975, 1987, 1999, 2011, 2023, 2035

A gentle artist of life / harmony and inner peace as ideals
Strengths: sensitive, tactful, empathetic, graceful, strong-willed
Weaknesses: conflict averse, moody, indifferent

The mission of the rabbit is to bring beauty into the world. Harmony and inner peace is very important to him and his subtle nature allows him to see behind the facades. Quarrels are alien to him and superficialities do not interest him. He is graceful, gentle and sensitive, often seems a bit inscrutable and yet knows exactly what he wants. He is characterized by prudence, composure and tact. Family means a lot to him. Everyday chores, however, are not his thing.

February

CW 7	≈	*Aquarius* 20.01. – 18.02.
Mon 12	☾ ☽	Rose Monday, ✝ *The return of the lost son*, St. Eulalia
Tue 13	♂ ☽	Carnival ╎ *Γαμηλιών* ╎
Wed 14	☿ ☽	Ash Wednesday, St. Valentine (Valentine's Day) **H** *Vasant Panchami (Odisha)*
Thu 15	♃ ☽	**B** *Parinirvana Day*
Fri 16	♀ ☽	half moon waxing, Feast of the goddess Hecate
Sat 17 -	♄ ☽	
Sun 18 +	☉ ☽	St. Simon

~ 27 ~

Goddess Hecate: Queen of the witches

The first annual festival of the goddess Hecate (Heqit, Heket) celebrates the merging of all seven Hathors. Hecate is the Greek goddess of crossroads, thresholds and transitions, of transformation, sorcery and magic. She is the guardian of the gates between the worlds, goddess of earth and life, growth, and is also known as the goddess of death. The Greek poet Hesiod described her as a helpful goddess who, along with Zeus, is the only deity who can grant or deny people any wish. The sacred symbol of Hecate is the toad or frog, both symbols of conception and procreation. So she is also goddess of midwifery and patroness of midwives. Hecate in her triple appearance as Selene, Artemis and Persephone has been worshipped as the Great Mother since the beginning of Greek mythology. The Egyptian Heka are the words of power, the magic words that bring into being or destroy. Hecate is the personified magic of the word and is revered as the queen of witches.

Prayer to Hecate

Hecate, Hecate, Hecate!
Goddess of the swamp and the willow.
Divine, wise old bringer of death!
Queen of the night, of the dark moon.
Mistress of shadows, daughter of Mordul.
Let us enter your world that we may know you.
We bring libations and offerings.
Show us your dark face, your bloody, wise secret.
Lead us into the shadows, into the dark night.
We call you, we call you!

Witch symbol: Hecate's wheel

"Hecate's Wheel" is a very famous witch symbol and most popular among the witchcraft communities led by women. It contains the three aspects of the triple goddess (virgin, mother and old woman). Hecate is the goddess of magic and sorcery and also the goddess of crossroads.

The three parts of the labyrinth represented in the symbol symbolize the three phases of femininity and the crossroads that every woman goes through to enter these three phases of life, coupled with the power and knowledge she gains from each phase. Thus, "Hekate's Wheel" is mainly used in rituals involving transformation, change, strengthening of feminine power and knowledge.

February

CW 8		**Pisces** 19.02. – 20.03.
	♓	🌲 *Pine - Tree of patience:* 19. – 29.02.
Mon 19	☾	Pisces > 20.03.
	●	
Tue 20	♂	World Day of Social Justice
	●	
Wed 21	☿	St. Felix
	●	
Thu 22 -	♃	St. Peter's Day
	●	
Fri 23	♀	
	●	
Sat 24	♄	full moon: Snow Moon
	○	
Sun 25	☉	St. Wallburga
	●	

February Full Moon

Snow Moon

Since the Native American Indigenous observe that there
is the heaviest snowfall in North America at this time,
they call the full moon in February "Snow Moon."

Witch symbol: Triskele

The triskele (triple spiral) is an ancient Celtic symbol that also appeared
in many other cultures. The name is of Greek origin and means "three-legged".

The triskele is a symbol of the circle of life: birth, life and death. Therefore,
it is also called the wheel of life and can relate to the past, the present and
the future. It also symbolizes progress and movement through the dynamics
of the spirals. This magical symbol is said to help harmonize body,
mind and spirit.

Ω ◇ Ω

*The one who follows logic
follows the deities.*

Pythagoras

Pisces 19.02. – 20.03.

The typical Pisces is friendly, empathetic, loving, dreamy, creative and emotional, but also chaotic, out of touch with reality, gullible, sentimental.

Good time for magical work around the themes of clairvoyance, telepathy, dreams, music and creative arts.

Planets: Zeus (Jupiter) and Poseidon (Neptune) / **Angel:** Sachiel / **Olympian spirit:** Bethor / **Element:** water / **Lucky stones:** coral, turquoise, aquamarine / **Colors:** purple, gray, blue, river green, white / **Lucky Day:** Thursday / **Lucky numbers:** 4, 14, 24 / **Flowers:** iris, camellia, jasmine, hibiscus, poppy / **Metal:** pewter / **Animals:** elephant, dolphin, dog, water birds, fish species / **Body parts influenced:** feet, toes, lungs and everything in the body that has to do with liquid

Pisces in 2024

The predictions for 2024 indicate for you that there will be changes in your interpersonal relationships, possibly also in your partnership. You will meet new people, your self-confidence will increase and you will dare new ventures. Despite difficult external circumstances, you will have the opportunity this year to implement firm decisions for your future. Here you will get support, on which you can rely rock solid, from your close environment. This will give you security, stability and confidence. In 2024 you will experience significant changes and tackle difficult issues. The year begins with nervousness and moodiness. Ares in Gemini brings some restructuring in January in the family, at home and / or in the professional sphere. There will be tensions in the family environment, especially at the beginning of the year, but from April they will be less and finally can be settled completely.

In your professional life, you will face some challenges, but you will overcome them with tact and balance. In the last five years you have gone through considerable restructuring, but you have managed to persist and even improve in your profession. Under the influence of the general developments, you have matured quite a bit as people and have learned to cooperate patiently with the system, to be consistent and to deal with difficult obligations. You are entering a time of responsibility, pressure to perform, and hard work. You realize that nothing is given to you and that efficient and well-planned work is necessary. You must not leave anything to chance or set your goals too high.

In the period from 01. January to 20. February, when you feel the influence of Zeus in Aries, your finances will be better off than before and opportunities will reveal themselves to further improve your financial situation through additional sources of income. Also, you will manage to buy something you have wanted for a very long time. You will have a long way to go to achieve stability in your life and realize your dreams. Nevertheless, remain optimistic and take advantage of every opportunity that comes your way.

In 2024, you will grow and develop through your determination. You will have as much time as you need to fix the things that have gone wrong in your life so far. However, this will require a lot of self-discipline and a well-thought-out plan of action. Don't doubt your abilities, even if others don't believe in you and your success and even talk badly about you behind your back. You know yourself best. Listen to yourself and your gut feeling and go your way with determination. This way you will be able to lay solid foundations for the rest of your life.

Pisces: love, family and friends

2024 presents you with countless gifts of love and helps you achieve your desires in your love life! Uranus brings for you sudden confessions of love as well as exciting acquaintances. Especially in April and May sensuality and stability characterize your feelings and in summer love and great passion play a very important role in your life. Singles the year brings many carefree flirtations and also those who live in a firm partnership may look forward to many a joyful surprise in love. And indeed, 2024 is a very good year for Pisces-born people who live in a long-distance relationship. Your love at a distance will flourish especially well this year. The kilometers separating you from your partner will not get in the way of your feelings, but on the contrary will strengthen them. 2024 is also a year for you to revitalize your existing partnership, for example through more togetherness and clarifying discussions and possibly even with the help of partnership counseling. However, relationships that have drifted apart to such an extent that it is no longer possible to get closer will not continue to ripple along. 2024 gives such relationships the impetus to separate and make a new start in love.

However, 2024 warns you not to get involved anew with a past love. It also advises you to evaluate your love realistically and avoid romantic idealizations. The solar eclipses in April and October make you jealous and very demanding.

Very important for you in 2024 is harmony in your family circle. Focus on the members of your family and a good togetherness. However, you should give up some responsibility in the family area. You cannot take care of everything.

Maintain your relationships with your close, trusted friends who can support you through difficult situations in your life. Expand your social circle. You may also join groups that advocate human rights, because the increasing discrimination in society will bother you especially this year.

Pisces: profession and finances

Your financial income will improve noticeably in 2024. You will excel at everything you set out to do, while generating a stable income for you and your family. Fundamental decisions and the need to change the rhythm of your life will play an important role. 2024 requires discipline and consistency in everything you start with enthusiasm.

You will find support from third parties, achieve success in commercial activities, especially in the spring and summer, and strengthen financial partnerships that will play a significant role in the next three years. By May, you may feel that some of these partnerships are not paying off, but your patience will pay off. From July to September, you can settle pending legal matters, as well as take advantage of opportunities that come your way on a professional level. Summer and the beginning of autumn are the most suitable time for important professional and financial decisions and good investments.

Finances are a big area that you should pay special attention to in 2024. The opportunities to get money will be numerous, but the temptations to spend it right away will be just as numerous. During the period from February to April, 2024 will help you find new ways to improve your income. You will experience how your wallet gradually fills up and you will successfully invest and invest your money profitably. However, be sure to avoid exposing yourself to financial risks during the period around the eclipses, and instead take care of the management and security of your money.

2024 gives you the impetus to steer your professional life in the right direction. Your self-confidence at work grows and you take off with your career. You know what you want and how to get it. Don't settle for less. Even if you have to compete with people who envy your position, you have the ability and the assertiveness to demand what is rightfully yours. But also positively influence the people who look up to you through exemplary work and behavior.

Pisces: health

As for health, the planets don't seem to be particularly aligned in your favor in 2024. So you need to take good care of yourself. Take the necessary precautions and then you will be fine. Make sure you take time for yourself to rest, relax and have fun. Outings with friends and your loved one(s) will help strengthen your psyche and keep you balanced. In 2024, you often feel like you are carrying a heavy load. You have many obligations that increasingly burden you. Starting in the spring, you will have to deal with exhaustion. Shift down a gear and listen to your body and tired mind. Reflect on what you have already accomplished and allow yourself times to pause and recharge your batteries.

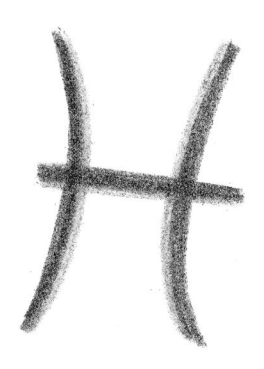

February / March

CW 9	♓	**Pisces** *19.02. – 20.03.*
		🌿 *Willow – Tree of vitality: 01. - 10.03.*
Mon 26	☾ ●	St. Alexander
Tue 27	♂ ●	† Ανθεστήρια †
Wed 28	☿ ●	St. Romanus † Χόες †
Thu 29	♃ ●	
Fr 1	♀ ◐	Matronalia (Festival of the women)
Sat 2	♄ ◐	
Sun 3 +	☉ ◐	**half moon waning**, World Wildlife Day, † *Triodion (Trinity) begins*

Monthly trend March	love	friends, family	profession, money
Aries	☼☼	☼☼☼☼☼	☼☼☼☼☼
Taurus	☼☼☼	☼☼☼☼☼	☼☼☼☼☼
Gemini	☼☼☼☼☼	☼☼☼☼☼	☼☼☼☼☼
Cancer	☼☼☼☼☼	☼☼☼☼☼	☼☼☼
Leo	☼☼☼	☼☼☼☼	☼☼☼☼☼
Virgo	☼☼☼☼	☼☼☼☼☼	☼☼☼
Libra	☼☼	☼☼	☼☼☼☼☼
Scorpio	☼☼☼☼	☼☼	☼☼
Sagittarius	☼☼	☼☼☼☼☼	☼
Capricorn	☼☼☼☼☼	☼	☼☼☼☼☼
Aquarius	☼☼	☼☼☼☼☼	☼☼☼☼☼
Pisces	☼☼☼☼	☼☼☼	☼☼

Suitable tools for magical processes

Magical processes work even better when the corresponding essential oils, herbs, incense, gemstones and colors are used.

Help you to creativity and inspiring ideas
Essential oils: lilac, jasmine, rose - **Herbs:** rose petals - **Incense:** lilac, lotus flower, rose - **Gemstones:** onyx, lapis lazuli, turquoise - **Colors:** yellow, purple

Help your unhappy partnership to new impulses
Essential oil: rose - **Herbs:** rose petals - **Incense:** clove pepper, sandalwood - **Gemstones:** lapis lazuli, amethyst, rose agate, diamond - **Color:** pink

Win the love of a man
Essential oils: vanilla, apple blossom - **Herbs:** ginger - **Incense:** vanilla, YlangYlang - **Gemstones:** magnetite, aventurine, malachite - **Color:** red

Win the love of a woman
Essential oil: white musk - **Herbs:** rose petals - **Incense:** jasmine, rose - **Gemstones:** magnetite, coral, pink quartz - **Color:** pink

Banish an unwanted lover from your life
Essential oil: patchouli - **Herbs:** lemon bush, verbena, cayenne pepper - **Incense:** rue - **Gemstones:** nephrite, quartz, agate, malachite - **Color:** black

Ω *Many more magic processes and their matching tools can be found in the great Witchbook (info on this on pages 156 / 157)*

March

CW 10	♓	*Pisces* 19.02. – 20.03.
Mon 4	☾	
Tue 5	♂	World Day of Prayer
Wed 6	☿	
Thu 7	♃	St. Felicitas
Fri 8	♀	International Women's Day
Sat 9 +	♄	† *Saturday of the souls*
Sun 10	☉	**new moon**, 40 Martyrs (40 Knights)

~ 36 ~

Divination arts

There are very diverse magical arts in the broad field of divination. Probably the best known is **Tasseography**: the interpretation of coffee grounds or tea leaves. Looking into the future with the help of **wax and metal casting (Ceromancy and Molybdomancy)** or even the **Egg oracle (Ovomancy)** are other, not quite so common methods. Here is an overview of these three arts of divination:

The Tasseography

Two very widespread methods of fortune telling are the interpretation of coffee grounds or tea leaves, also called Tasseography or Tasseomancy. Often these two terms are used only in connection with tea leaf interpretation, but sometimes they are used as an umbrella term for both divination techniques. The interpretation of coffee grounds has a long tradition. In the 14th century, coffee arrived in Arabia from its namesake region of origin, Kaffa in Ethiopia. The Yemeni city of Mocha was then soon considered the capital of coffee and from here the art of coffee grounds interpretation spread. Since time immemorial, people have been fascinated by the idea of making predictions and forecasts about the future. And the interpretation of coffee grounds is an easy-to-learn method. It offers especially coffee lovers a good opportunity to try fortune telling once.

For the interpretation of the coffee grounds themselves, there are no strict rules. What matters is your energy and your intuitive ability to interpret the symbols and the messages from the coffee correctly. When coffee grounds or even tea leaves are read intuitively, they are about images that make you think and feel. A bell, for example, can mean a message of an upcoming wedding as well as a funeral. So you have to decide for yourself, trust your intuition. You will, if you are more practiced, see in your coffee cup really incredible and often hair-precisely depicted and detailed signs, just as if a master painter or an artistic oversized intelligence was at work.

A sitting wolf and opposite him an eagle on a rock. The wolf often indicates hostility towards us. The sitting eagle with closed wings is an image of security and prosperity. Interpreted together, the Tasseography image could advise us to take good care of our possessions. It could be threatened.

The Ceromancy and Molybdomancy

Ceromancy (Candle Oracle, Wax Casting) and Molybdomancy (Metal Oracle, Lead Casting) are branches of the ancient divination art of Pyromancy (Fire Oracle), which dates back to ancient times. These rather unknown divination arts can actually predict even serious events and require deep respect both in the preparation and in the execution itself.

Ceromancy and Molybdomancy are directly related to fire. Fire purifies everything and is one of the most powerful elements of our matrix. Ceromancy and Molybdomancy know many methods of divination.

For some, the images of the candle flame used to melt the wax or metal are included in the interpretation. Others focus only on interpreting the cooled forms that emerge after casting into the water. But each method makes use of fire. Ceromancy was and is practiced in many countries of the world. For example, in Poland, on 30. November, the name day of Saint Andrew. He is seen as the proclaimer of the future, which is why many Oracle rituals have always been practiced on this day. Wax casting in particular is still very popular on this day. Many of these Andreas Oracles concern, how could it be otherwise, love of course. But since the Middle Ages, people have also used Wax Oracles to try to uncover crimes, such as theft. To do this, they melted wax and spoke special magic words before pouring it over glowing coals. In the later cooled creations they searched for indications. With a very important ritual of Ceromancy, which is deeply rooted in witchcraft and is still practiced today, it is possible to find out who or what is responsible for a sudden suffering, illness and / or a streak of bad luck.

The Ovomancy

Egg Oracle, also called Ovomancy, Oomancy or Ooscopy, is the art of divining and prophesying future events by interpreting the characteristics of eggs and their individual components (shell, albumen, yolk). Ovomancy describes the art of gaining knowledge about the future from an egg. For this purpose, countless symbols, which the egg reveals about the present, past and future, are included in the prophecy. Ovomancy is a very old art. Its roots go back to the beginning of human history and it has been passed down from generation to generation. It knows very many variations, even one in which the unbroken hard-boiled egg was interpreted. Although this magical form of divination has evolved greatly over many centuries, very few people actually master it today and are often unwilling to share the secrets of this divination art.

Traditionally, Egg Oracles were performed on feast days in honor of Aphrodite, Selene or Hecate, on Walpurgis Night, on the two days of the solstice, on Mabon, and in many parts of the world also on New Year's Eve and on the commemoration day of St. John the Baptist (29. August). And of course to Ostara! Because the Egg Oracle is directly related to the Easter tradition of coloring eggs (usually red for the blood of Jesus Christ) and giving them away.

You can get answers to questions from all areas of life with the help of the Egg Oracle – whether it concerns finances, career, love, partnership and family or pregnancy and birth. Since the egg is considered a symbol of fertility, just the determination of the sex of an unborn child or the number of babies in the womb was and is a frequent topic at the Egg Oracle. Also whether there will be possible complications during birth is a frequently asked question in Ovomancy. Eggs, however, can also be used for a very general look into the future, but in this case they must be examined in a different way.

If you want to go deeper into the divination arts of Tasseography, Ceromancy, Molybdomancy and Ovomancy, these books on the subject are for you. In addition to detailed instructions on how to learn these arts, they contain great rituals, many illustrated examples of interpretation and a large lexicon with over 700 symbols.

March

CW 11	♓	**Pisces** *19.02. – 20.03.*
		🌿 **Linden tree – Tree of harmony:** *11. - 20.03.*
Mon 11	☾	
Tue 12 +	♂	St. Gregor
Wed 13 -	☿	
Thu 14 +	♃	† Tsiknopempti (Smoke Thursday, Consumption of meat)
Fri 15	♀	
Sat 16 +	♄	
Sun 17	☉	half moon waxing

March

CW 12	♈	**Aries** 21.03. - 20.04. (previously Pisces)
		🌿 **Oak – Tree of strength:** 21.03. /
		🌿 **Hazel – Tree of truth:** 22. - 31.03.
Mon 18	☾	† *Kathara Deftera – Radiant (clean) Monday* *I Shab-e-Barat / Lailatu l-Bara'a – Night of Forgiveness (+ 19.03.)*
Tue 19 -	♂	St. Joseph
Wed 20	☿	**Ostara**, equinox, beginning of spring, International Day of Happiness
Thu 21	♃	World Poetry Day, **Aries** > 20.04. International Day for the Elimination racial discrimination, St. Benedict, St. Lupicinius
Fri 22	♀	World Water Day
Sat 23 -	♄	*J Esther Fast - Ta'anit Esther, Purim (+ 24.03.)*
Sun 24	☉	Lunar eclipse (penumbral, Mar 24 > 25), † Ἐλαφηβόλια † Palm Sunday, Archangel Gabriel, † *Sunday of Orthodoxy (1st Sunday of Lent)*

~ 41 ~

Ostara 20. *March*

Ostara marks the beginning of spring. The Goddess has extended her blessings to all creation and everything has blossomed. God is teenager and is happy to express his energy in the blooming meadows and forests. All animals are encouraged to mate to ensure their continued existence. The Renaissance is celebrated in all its glory. It is a time of new beginnings and also a time to start gardening and plant the first (medicinal) herbs. It is also a good time to detoxify the body (for example with alkaline herbal teas) and to fast.

Probably the most famous custom for Easter, when Christians celebrate the resurrection of Jesus, is the Easter egg, painting eggs. This Custom has its origin in all pagan traditions and comes from ancient Egypt and Mesopotamia. The reason for this was that on 21. March most ancient civilizations celebrated the New Year.

The egg from antiquity was one of the main symbols of the Renaissance. People painted magical symbols of regeneration, protection and fertility on eggs with intense colors obtained from plants and placed them on altars as sacrifices to the goddess of Mother Earth. **It is also equinox and the sun is 0 degrees in Aries.**

Egg oracle ritual at Ostara or on the day of the Easter moon

Light **a bright candle** on the day of the Easter Full Moon and place it on your altar. **It is best to choose the planetary hours of Selene for this ritual.** Place **a transparent glass with fresh water in which you have put a few drops of an essential oil with a protective effect** (for example sage, rosemary or gum resin) next to it. Finally, lay **a fresh, raw egg** on it. Cleanse the room with **incense** (preferably also sage, rosemary or gum resin).

Now hold the glass of water in your hands and ask Ostara for protection and guidance. Do the same with the egg. Now take the egg in your hand and gradually roll it over your whole body, starting around the head, then over the face, neck, both arms, chest and belly, then the back (as you are able) and the front and back of both legs. Finally, roll the egg over your hand palms and the soles of your feet. Make sure you always move the egg clockwise and down towards the floor. Take your time. It is important that you perform the ritual (like any ritual) in a calm, relaxed state.

Then break the shell of the egg and let the yolk and egg white flow into the water glass. Observe the egg in the water closely for a while: Look for the smell, the color, the shapes it melts into and whether there are any bloody traces in the yolk. Fix your gaze straight on the yolk and look for possible characters, numbers or letters, for example.

If you even recognize the face of a certain person, then this person sends negative energy to you or robs you of power (the well-known energy vampire). If you recognize an eye in the center of the yolk, this is the infamous "evil eye". With both images (face and eyes) you should cleanse yourself spiritually and take protective measures if necessary.

On the other hand, if you see small air bubbles rising in the water around the egg, it is a very good sign. Deities and other heavenly beings protect you and stand by you to solve your problems. If the water is clear and clean and does not give off an unpleasant smell, then there was no magical work against you.

Thank Ostara for her divine assistance and protection. Bury the egg away from the house and garden somewhere in the wild, regardless of whether the ritual showed you good or bad.

Ω *More magical rituals related to this divination art can be found in the book "Egg Oracle – Ovomancy, Oomancy, Ooscopy" (info on this on pages 162 / 163).*

Ω ⟐ Ω

*In years of tyranny, the people are like worms,
which is trampled underfoot.
In years of democracy
it is like a bear devouring its leaders.*
Pythagoras

Aries 21.03. – 20.04.

Typical for the Aries are drive and the need to win. Aries-born people are direct, decisive and ruthless.

Good time for magical work related to willpower, leadership and rebirth

Planets: Ares (Mars) and Hades (Pluto) / **Angel:** Samael / **Olympian spirit:** Phaleg / **Element:** fire / **Lucky stones:** diamond, ruby, red jasper, amethyst / **Colors:** red, orange, fiery colors / **Lucky day:** Tuesday / **Lucky numbers:** 7, 47, 87 / **Flowers:** carnation, poppy, tulip / **Metal:** iron / **Animals:** wolf, predators, mustang, big cats / **Body part influenced:** head

Aries in 2024

In the course of 2024, your priorities in life change: What was once very important to you loses importance and new things are now in focus for you. 2024 promises significant changes both at work and in love. Much in your life will take a new shape and especially at the beginning of the year you can expect revelations, scandals as well as power and dominance struggles. Important events happen that will determine your further path in life. Cronos confronts you relentlessly with past actions and events for which you were responsible. He thus brings your fears and insecurities to your attention. You will be ready to face great challenges in order to achieve your lofty goals. Even though things will change for the better in your life, you should be careful not to make mistakes that will have a lasting effect on your life.

The past year 2023 was bittersweet for you, as Cronos imposed many a hard test on you on the one hand, but Zeus brought some beautiful things into your life on the other. In 2024 you will reap what you have sown the year before by your decisions. Now you see more clearly for your future life path. You bring order to your thoughts and manage to control and finally overcome your fears.

The beginning of 2024 is most suitable for you to enter into a new partnership, but you have to proceed with empathy here and by no means want to go through the wall with your head. Cronos will still be in the zodiac sign of Pisces well into 2025 and so his influence on you in 2024 is strong. Starting in the spring, you will be challenged to face problems that you have been disregarding. Start putting your ideas into action. Stay true to yourself and do things that make you truly happy. The planet Ares, which matches your zodiac sign, will help you change your views on life. Stop paying so much attention to the opinions of others and take care of your own needs and desires.

2024 will be a blessed year for you. Therefore, you should take advantage of every opportunity that comes your way in the best possible way for you. Trust your abilities. You can now complete projects that have long lain dormant in the drawer without any significant obstacles, almost with ease. Only the times around the eclipses will bring isolated difficulties and test your patience and nerves.

Aries: love, family and friends

Those in a committed partnership or marriage will face a tough test at the beginning of 2024. You will experience some adversity and face great challenges that may even lead to the breakup of the relationship. However, if you are determined and also sure that your partner is the person you want to grow old with, then you will have a chance to strengthen your relationship after surviving the crisis. From March, your love life will change for the better. However, jealousy will cause tension in the times of eclipses. The singles among Aries will find it easier to fall in love in 2024. You will be surrounded by people who like you and would like to be a part of their lives. However, do not rush into anything. First be quite sure who you want to open your heart to. In fact, it is also very possible that you will rekindle a romantic relationship from the past that was once very important to you.

For a long time you have neglected your family. It is important to make up for lost time with them this year if you want to achieve balance in your life. You may have to make some changes to be able to be there more for your family. Keep your promise and fulfill your responsibilities to your loved ones. 2024 is a year of many changes for you. For this time of change, surround yourself primarily with people who will support and advance you mentally and spiritually, and on whom you can rely. You will realize that you need to expand your social contacts so that you don't just revolve around yourself and your own experiences.

Aries: profession and finances

For many of you, the financial situation will improve significantly, whether due to an inheritance or an increase in income. Freelancers can look forward to increased sales due to a rising order situation. So you definitely won't have any money worries in 2024. On the contrary, you will enjoy financial abundance. The money will flow continuously for you. But plan your investments prudently and with foresight. The best time for this is February and March, and also take into account any payment obligations, such as loans, so that you do not get into a financial mess despite the flow of money. Rather, create reserves for the future. From September onwards, you will benefit from financial partnerships you have entered into. However, minor financial setbacks due to possessiveness are possible around the lunar eclipses in March, September and October. For those who want to make a career change in 2024, the most likely period to do so is from late April to late May. However, you should have made preparations for this beforehand and also thoroughly consider what you want for your professional future and what you are prepared to give up for it.

Aries: health

Your desire for more money will make you work more, possibly even two jobs in parallel. This will leave you little time to rest or to balance your work with exercise and sports. This will weaken your health. Especially in the period from March to July, pay close attention to a healthy diet, and in April and May, avoid hasty actions and anything that has to do with speed so as not to injure yourself.

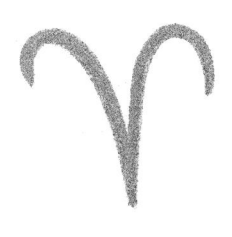

March

CW 13	♈	*Aries* 21.03. – 20.04.
Mon 25	☾ ◐	full moon: **Worm Moon**, Feast of Maria's Annunciation, Greek Independence Day, **H** *Holi Festival – Doljatra*
Tue 26	♂ ●	
Wed 27	☿ ●	St. Rupert
Thu 28 -	♃ ●	Maundy Thursday
Fri 29	♀ ●	**Good Friday** (Jesus' crucifixion), St. Berthold
Sat 30	♄ ●	Holy Saturday
Sun 31	☉ ◐	**Easter** (Jesus' resurrection), Beginning of summer time

March Full Moon
Worm Moon

The Native American Indigenous call the full moon in March "Worm Moon," because in this month the snow melts and the birds pull the first earthworms out of the thawed ground.

Use the power of the moon

The full moon

The night of the full moon gives strength to desires for strength, ambition and success. Also each of the three days before and after the full moon are under its influence and are therefore suitable for rituals on these topics. The time around full moon is also the ideal time for **rituals for love, protection, divination and inner purification.** The power of the full moon can also strengthen any holistic therapy.

The day immediately after the full moon is called the Dark or Black Moon (Lilith time) and it is an extremely powerful and very dangerous moment. Incantations and rituals involving hatred and enmity are performed then. Black magicians practice their aggressive magic, which can cause, for example, divorces, earthquakes, disasters or diseases. In magic there are countless rituals for this time, which have to do with everything we want to remove from our lives.
In fact, the power of the Dark Moon is also suitable for renouncing black magic.

The new moon

The new moon is the time when the moon is not visible in the night sky. Although we do not see the moon during this phase for three days or nights, the new moon actually lasts only a single brief moment. At new moon the energy is on the side facing away from us. **During this time, protection rituals and everything that requires secrecy gain special strength. We can use this time** – as in the waning phase before – **to remove negative elements from our lives.** New moon is also the **ideal time for all magical work related to creativity and new beginnings.**
The new moon works beneficially when we have to deal with the pain of losing a loved one.

The energy of the new moon gives the power to finally close an old circle before we want to make a new beginning. New moon is also **the ideal time for planning strategic steps, making final decisions and rejecting situations that we no longer want to have.**

April

CW 14	♈	**Aries** *21.03. – 20.04.* 🌾 ***Mountain ash – Tree of vitality:*** *01. - 10.04.*
Mo 1	☾	Easter Monday
Tue 2	♂	half moon waning, St. Ezekiel, St. Rosamunde
Wed 3	☿	St. Chrestus, St. Pappus
Thu 4	♃	
Fri 5 +	♀	*I Lailat al-Qadr (Night of Destiny)*
Sat 6	♄	
Sun 7	☉	World Health Day

Monthly trend April	love	friends, family	profession, money
Aries	☼☼	☼☼☼☼☼☼	☼☼☼☼☼
Taurus	☼☼☼☼☼☼	☼☼☼☼☼	☼
Gemini	☼☼☼☼☼☼	☼	☼☼☼☼
Cancer	☼☼	☼☼☼☼☼☼	☼☼
Leo	☼☼☼☼☼☼	☼☼☼	☼☼☼☼☼☼
Virgo	☼	☼☼☼☼☼☼	☼☼☼☼
Libra	☼☼☼☼☼☼	☼☼☼	☼☼
Scorpio	☼☼	☼☼☼☼☼☼	☼☼☼☼☼☼
Sagittarius	☼☼☼☼☼☼	☼☼☼	☼☼☼☼☼☼
Capricorn	☼☼	☼☼☼☼☼☼	☼☼
Aquarius	☼☼☼☼☼☼	☼	☼☼
Pisces	☼☼☼☼☼☼	☼☼☼☼☼☼	☼☼

Witch symbols:
Celtic knot and All-seeing eye

The Celtic knot is an ancient symbol of protection, of which there are countless variations. Besides the protective aspect, it is often used to ward off negativity. Among the Celts, it was also the symbol of birth, life and death, the elements of earth, air and water, and also femininity.

The All-seeing eye (an eye surrounded by sun rays) is a powerful symbol of protection. The triangle in which it is usually represented stands for the Trinity.

April

CW 15	♈	**Aries** 21.03. - 20.04.
		Maple – Tree of freedom: 11. - 20.04.
Mon 8	☾ ☉	new moon, solar eclipse (total)
Tue 9	♂ ☾	*I Eid – end of Ramadan (+ 10.04.)* † Ιλάρια †
Wed 10	☿ ☾	St. Ezekiel
Thu 11	♃ ☾	
Fri 12	♀ ☾	
Sat 13	♄ ☾	St. Martin
Sun 14	☉ ☾	

April

CW 16	♉	**Taurus** *21.04. – 20.05.* (previously Aries)
		🌿 ***Walnut – Tree of new beginnings:*** *21. - 30.4.*
Mon 15	☾	half moon waxing
Tue 16	♂	
Wed 17 +	☿	
Thu 18 -	♃	† *Great Liturgy of St. Raphael, St. Nicholas and St. Irene*
Fri 19	♀	
Sat 20 -	♄	
Sun 21	☉	† *Life-giving spring Mother of God,* **Taurus > 20.05.** *Ridvan Festival – Baha'i (until 02.05.)*

Taurus 21.04. – 20.05.

Reliability, sensuality and practical disposition are the characteristics of the Taurus. However, he can also be stubborn and possessive.

Good time for magic work, that with finances, real estate and love

Planet: Aphrodite (Venus) / **Angel**: Anael / **Olympian spirit**: Hagith / **Element**: earth / **Lucky stones**: emerald, turquoise, sapphire / **Colors**: pink, orange, bright green, earthy tones / **Lucky day**: Friday / **Lucky numbers**: 5, 25, 75 / **Flowers**: lily, hyacinth, rose, apple tree / **Metal**: copper / **Animals**: bull, seal, cow, buffalo, domestic dog, rhinoceros, horse / **Body parts influenced**: larynx, tonsils, teeth, ears, jaws

Taurus in 2024

In 2024, your doubts that have plagued you for at least the last four years by holding on to the past and preventing you from moving forward will end. Now, finally, you manage to come to terms with what has been and turn your gaze forward. 2024 marks the beginning of a new and interesting path for most people born under the zodiac sign of Taurus, one that will increase your vitality, optimism and performance. And very often the new path is in the area of love life. However, it is important that you completely work through and thus solve all the problems of the past, because otherwise they will catch up with you during the year and most likely around the time of the lunar and solar eclipses, and obstacles will arise on your new path in life. Also, do not overreach yourself in creating your new life. Tackle only as much as you can handle. Take care of yourself, but use your strong ability to communicate to inspire others with your ideas and get them on board. Together, many things are easier to achieve.

Meet life with a positive attitude. Change the way you see things around you. Be open to new things, be creative and innovative, and use your skills wisely. Be proactive and work to be productive in everything you do. 2024 challenges you to give your best. Laziness is out of place. Focus on your true desires and make a plan to achieve them. Listen to your heart and your gut feeling. Separate yourself from everything and everyone who does not suit you, even if this is often a hard step at first.

In the professional field, you will face some problems and it will require some effort on your part to solve them. But you will develop professionally. The year will end with good luck, as Zeus in your sign will help you to increase your income. Your health will be excellent for most of the year and you will enjoy a stable love life.

Taurus: love, family and friends

The year begins with several challenges and tensions for those in committed relationships. An affair that threatens to endanger the partnership, a marriage that has been postponed too long, or the announcement that there are offspring on the way may cause you to take responsibility more readily than in the past. Several times you will experience extreme situations in 2024. You must definitely try to react with understanding and de-escalation, otherwise you risk separation. Also, by putting aside your excessive pride and stop thinking that you are better than your partner, the problems in your relationship will be overcome.

Within the family, during the first three months of the year, the tensions that exist because of ideological differences will subside. The older members of the family will take the first step towards restoring peace, harmony and unity between them. 2024 heralds a time of new beginnings in your life, when you will make changes that are in the best interest of your family. And as long as your loved ones are happy, you will be too. However, avoid interference from your loved ones in your professional development. Set clear boundaries for family members in this area in particular.

You will also be confronted with changes in your circle of friends in 2024. It is possible that acquaintances will move to another city or country, or simply move on in a different direction and distance themselves from you in this way. Be careful that emotional outbursts cost you valuable friendships that you have built over the course of many years. There is no reason to hurt the people close to you with irrational behavior.

Taurus: profession and finances
Changes are also coming your way at a professional level in 2024. You will have the opportunity to expand your current area of responsibility. You will also be looking at entering into professional partnerships and cooperations that offer you the opportunity to change professions or make a career leap. These new challenges will help you mature. However, the path to your new position is not an easy one and will require some dedication and assertiveness on your part. You will build great relationships with the people you work with, and your superiors will be proud of your efforts and hard work and reward you accordingly.

You've had three years full of financial uncertainty that haven't let you rest easy. This will finally change in 2024. The planetary environment will now work in your favor, but you must act very prudently with your money, especially at the beginning of the year, and in no case make impulsive decisions. Once your financial situation stabilizes in the first half of the year, your plan to invest in real estate will take concrete shape. It is important that you are very careful with your spending and live only within your means. Spend your money only wisely settle your debts as soon as possible, if you have any.

Taurus: health
The overload of the past years has triggered an almost chronic exhaustion in you and you feel attacked both physically and psychologically. Your nerves are on edge and you have become very sensitive and quarrelsome. Make sure you eat healthy, get enough rest, exercise and sleep, even if you think you don't have time for it. Because otherwise you will have no strength to cope with all the tasks that are coming at you as a result of the changes in your life.

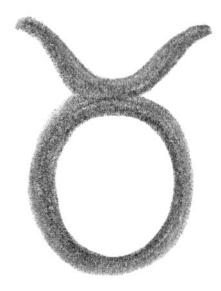

April

CW 17	♉	**Taurus** 21.04. – 20.05.
Mon 22	☾ ●	*J Erew Pesach – Seder Evening*, Earthday
Tue 23	♂ ●	† *Great Martyr St. Georg*, *J Passover (until 30.04)*, World Book Day
Wed 24	☿ ○	full moon: Pink Moon
Thu 25	♃ ●	
Fri 26	♀ ●	
Sat 27	♄ ●	† *Lazarus Day (Lazarus' resurrection)*, St. Peter Canisius
Sun 28	☉ ●	† *Palm Sunday*, St. Vital

April Full Moon
Pink Moon

The Native American Indigenous call the full moon in April "Pink Moon" because at this time of year the pink flame flowers bloom.

Witch symbol: Spiral goddess

With the spiral goddess, femininity is worshipped and she is used in rituals around the female aspects (sexuality, love, passion, female power, intuition, fertility, motherhood...). The spiral in the center of her belly also thematizes the aspects of creativity, emotions (Sacral Chakra) and the menstrual flow cycle.

Ω ◇ Ω

If you have a sore heart,
touch it as little as a sick eye.
There are only two medicines
for the pain of the soul:
hope and patience.
Pythagoras

April / May

CW 18	♉	**Taurus** 21.04. – 20.05.
		🍃 *Poplar – Tree of self-knowledge:* 01. - 14.05.
Mon 29 -	☾ ●	✝ Holy Monday
Tue 30 -	♂ ●	✝ Big Tuesday, **Walpurgis Night**
Wed 1 +	☿ ◐	half moon waning ✝ *Μουνιχιων* ✝ **Beltane**, Labor Day, mid-spring, ✝ Holy Wednesday, 💎 St. Philip Feast Day (San Felipe Pueblo)
Thu 2 +	♃ ☾	✝ **Great Thursday** (secret supper, Judas' betrayal, Jesus' arrest)
Fri 3	♀ ☾	✝ **Great Friday** *(Jesus Christ's crucifixion),* 💎 Santa Cruz Feast Day / Blessing of the Fields *(Taos Pueblo),* World Press Freedom Day
Sat 4 +	♄ ☾	✝ **Holy Saturday** *(Jesus Christ's entombment),* ✡ Yom haSho'a (+ 05.05.)
Sun 5	☉ ☾	✝ **Holy Easter / Anastase** *(Jesus Christ's resurrection),* ✝ St. Irene, St. Ephraim

Monthly trend May	love	friends, family	profession, money
Aries	☼☼☼☼☼	☼☼☼☼☼	☼☼☼☼☼
Taurus	☼☼	☼☼	☼☼☼☼☼
Gemini	☼	☼☼☼	☼☼☼
Cancer	☼	☼☼☼☼☼	☼☼☼☼
Leo	☼☼☼☼	☼☼☼☼☼	☼☼☼
Virgo	☼☼☼☼	☼☼☼☼☼	☼☼
Libra	☼☼☼☼☼	☼☼☼	☼☼
Scorpio	☼☼	☼☼☼☼☼	☼☼☼
Sagittarius	☼☼☼☼☼	☼☼☼☼☼	☼
Capricorn	☼☼	☼	☼☼
Aquarius	☼☼☼☼☼	☼☼☼☼☼	☼☼☼☼☼
Pisces	☼	☼	☼

Beltane 1. May

It is the most important festival in the faith of witches. On this day the sorcerers and witches all over the world celebrate: Eros! It is the day when God grows up and unites with the goddess Moon. The whole nature celebrates this union, everything is blossomed and the young girls wear on their heads a self-made wreath made of wild flowers and ask the divine couple to send them a partner. The festival is celebrated very exuberantly. The altar is decorated with colorful spring flowers and bands. The green stands for the Goddess, for God you can put up a small maypole. The ceremony is celebrated with incense, rose and lilac.

Beltane is usually celebrated on 01. May. However, there are some who celebrate this witchcraft festival around 05. May, when the sun in Taurus has reached the 15th degree. After Ostara, Beltane is the second festival of fertility and takes place in the middle of a blossoming, "exploding" nature. In the Irish calendar, Beltane marks the beginning of summer.

On Beltane, people light huge bonfires around which they dance or lead their animals to bless them and increase their fertility. A widely known custom is the dance around the maypole, which has its roots in the Olympic cult of Dionysus.

The maypole's stem is a phallic symbol, expressing the masculine power of the heaven (God). The wreath on top symbolizes the vulva, the feminine power of the earth (Goddess). So when the feminine and masculine unite, it is Beltane, a celebration of fertility, pleasure, sensuality and passion. So Beltane rituals often include sexual activity, sometimes even veritable orgies. Childless couples decide in such an orgy of love that the fertile partner unites with a likewise fertile ritual participant. It is strengthening, if the person giving life later actually takes over the spiritual godparenthood for the child conceived during the ritual.

It is said that these Beltane children have a very great psychic power and love for the world and nature. In earlier times, they were even seen as belonging to the gods. However, Beltane is also about spiritual fertility and creativity. So this festival is the perfect time to work magic for growth and abundance or to increase your sexual libido.

The 7 Knots Love Ritual

With this ritual you can try to win a partner for yourself or also to win back a lost love. The ritual is best practiced in the phase of the waxing moon and in the times of Aphrodite, which means on a Friday and if possible also in one of her planetary hours on that day.

What you need
- ☆ Incense that goes with Aphrodite (myrtle, amber, aloe wood)
- ☆ 2 red Adam and Eve candles
- ☆ a handful of red rosebuds
- ☆ 1 little thicker cord (about 30 cm long)
- ☆ 1 photo of the potential partner (if possible)

Adam and Eve candles from SPIRITUAL ART

Start with the incense and light the two candles. Then add the cord, the rosebuds and the picture of the desired partner, if you have one. Focus your eyes on the picture of the partner or visualize it in your mind. Now take the rosebuds and enclose them tightly with both hands.

Now close your eyes and imagine your life with your partner as accurately as possible. Feel all your desires, give free play to your emotions and hold nothing back. The more precisely you can create your desired partner, your secret wishes for this love, the surroundings in which you want to live with him or her, the stronger the effect of the ritual.

Now take the cord and hold it in the incense for a short time to strengthen its magical power. Then start tying 7 knots in the cord. With each knot, say the following words:

Holy goddess of love, Aphrodite, I ask you:
Let (name of partner) **no longer find peace or**
feel pleasure until his / her heart beats only for me!
All the roads he / she walks along shall lead only to me!
Holy goddess of love, Aphrodite, stand by me and
***bring** (name of partner)* **to me / back to me!**

Now take the 7-fold knotted cord and hold it over the incense again. The ritual is completed. Keep everything safe in a secret place to which no one else has access. Do this ritual 5 days in a row, each time during the hours of Aphrodite. Afterwards, keep everything safe again. The ritual is very powerful and usually shows its effects quickly. You may be able to enjoy your new / old love very soon. Be patient for about a month. If the Higher Powers do not approve your ritual, then you can repeat the ritual again after this time has passed!

When the ritual has been successful, it is very important to complete it as follows: Light the two candles again and burn "Aphrodite incense". Now burn in the candle flames the knotted cord, the rosebuds and also the picture of the partner. While doing this you say these words:

Holy goddess of love, Aphrodite,
I thank you for your help!
Let me and (name of partner) find our peace
and live our love with dignity forever!
Holy goddess of love, Aphrodite,
I offer you these rosebuds, the 7-knot cord
and the picture of my beloved.
My prayer of thanks,
carried by the incense,
shall reach you high above in the Olympus!
Holy goddess Aphrodite, stand by me always!

Put the remains in a metal bowl and burn it together with the candle remains so that nothing is left but ashes. It is best to spread these in the open countryside.

May

CW 19	♉	**Taurus** 21.04. – 20.05.
Mon 6 +	☽ ☾	☦ *Ederlezi Roma spring festival in honor of St. George*
Tue 7	♂ ☾	
Wed 8	☿ ☉	**new moon**, Day of remembrance and reconciliation for the victims of the 2nd World War
Thu 9 +	♃ ☽	**Ascension of Jesus Christ** (Father's Day)
Fri 10 -	♀ ☽	
Sat 11	♄ ☽	11. – 15.05. Ice Saints, St. Mamertus
Sun 12	☉ ☽	Mother's Day, St. Pankratius, **J** *Yom haAtzma'ut (+ 13.05.)*, **J** *Yom haZikaron (+ 13.05.)*

Witch symbol: Triangle

The triangle is one of the most important geometric shapes in spirituality. In Christianity it symbolizes the Holy Trinity (Father, Son and Holy Spirit). In other spiritual contexts it symbolizes the connection of body, mind and soul. The triangle can also stand for heaven, earth and man. The triangle with a circle inside it is very important for safety when summoning powerful and dangerous creatures.

Triangles for the elements

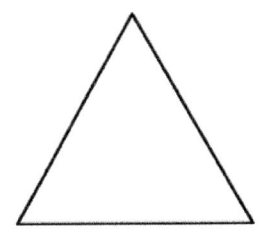

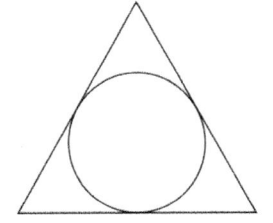

The triangle is also used as a sign for the five elements: earth, water, fire, air and ether.

The **element of fire** is represented in sacred geometry as a simple triangle. Fire is a symbol of light, warmth, but also power and the power of destruction. For witches and sorcerers this sign stands for activity, creativity, strength, power, courage and purifying energy. In rituals they use it to cleanse the space from negative energy and evil, creating new space for positive energy.

The symbol for the **element earth** is a downward pointing triangle, through which a line draws. This witch sign symbolizes Mother Earth, as well as the process of birth and life. It is used in rituals involving the female power, motherhood, fertility, growth and connection with the forces of nature.

The **element of water** is the opposite of the element of fire. Therefore, its symbol is a triangle standing on its tip. Water is the essence of life and necessary for life. As a witch symbol it stands for cleansing, purification and purification of the soul. The element of water plays a significant role in alchemy and esotericism, and that is why it can be found in almost all witchcraft rituals and spells. It is most often used when you want to attract feminine energy and something new.

The symbol for the **element air** is a triangle with a line. It is the sign of the soul and life. Air is present all around us, enveloping us and keeping us alive. However, it is elusive and constantly in motion. Therefore, it is a symbol of energy, vitality and change. For witches and sorcerers it symbolizes communication, reason and logic and they use it in rituals that are supposed to bring change or even better concentration.

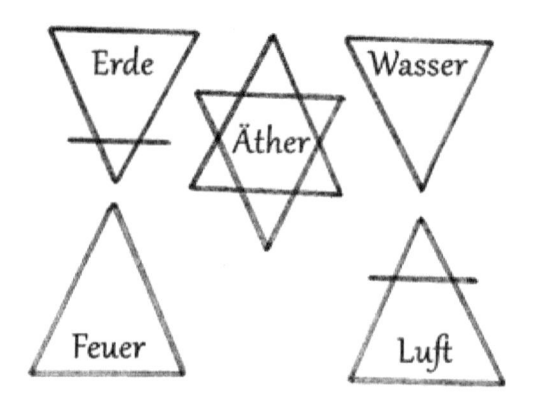

Finally, the hexagram is the symbol of the **element ether**. This is the union of the two polarities, the male and the female.
The ether is the spirit of all being and stands for transcendence and the eternal change. He is everything that was, is and will be.

While the elements earth, fire, water and air have a real correspondence and tangible reality, ether is a purely spiritual entity, but no less effective for that. Aether magic is only for experienced witches and sorcerers who have been practicing elemental magic for a long time and have mastered communication with the elemental spirits.

Ω ◇ Ω
As long as the humans stay
the restless destroyer of all life,
which he regards as lowly,
he will never know what health means,
he will never truly find peace.
Pythagoras

May

CW 20	♉	**Taurus** 21.04. – 20.05.
		🌿 **Chestnut – Tree of openness:** 15. - 24.05.
Mon 13	☾	💎 St. Anthony Feast Day (Sandia Pueblo), St. Servatius
Tue 14 +	♂	St. Matthias, St. Bonifaz
Wed 15	☿	half moon waxing, St. Sophia (Cold Sophia)
Thu 16	♃	St. Nepomuk, International Day of Light
Fri 17 -	♀	
Sat 18	♄	Feast of the god Pan
Sun 19	☉	Pentecost, Day of Commemoration of the Genocide of the Pontos Greeks

God Panas (Pan)

He is the shepherd god in Greek mythology. He is a hybrid of a human upper body and the lower body of a ram or a goat. There are several versions about the origin of the god Pan: The best-known myth names Hermes as his father and the nymph Dryope as his mother. He is also said to have been the inventor of the Pan flute: drunk with love, he pursued the beautiful nymph Syrinx, who, however, fled from him. At the river Ladon she turned into a reed, which Pan then embraced. The wind blew into the reed and plaintive sounds were heard. Pan did not want to lose these sounds and so he broke 7 parts from the reed, one always a little shorter than the previous one, and tied them together. So he invented the shepherd's flute, the Pan flute. Panas was also a great warrior and fought alongside the Greek Olympians in the Titan War and later against the Nephelim in the Giant War. He spread panic among the enemies and in fact the origin of the word "pan-ic" goes back to Pan.

Use the power of the moon:
The waxing moon

The phase when the moon is waxing lasts about 14 days. It begins with the new moon. When the moon is in the filling phase (period from the new moon to the full moon) it strengthens **all rituals related to one's own (spiritual) development, personal growth, health, love, knowledge and prosperity.** When the moon slowly fills, it is the ideal time for energy work, bringing **new beginnings,** and also **important for health, healing, fertility, outer beauty and strengthening spiritual and mental-mental forces.** Generally speaking, **the filling phase is suitable for all rituals that should bring positive influences or situations into our lives as well as banish all negative influences from it.** This period is even **suitable for repelling and neutralizing black magic.**

May

CW 21	♊	**Gemini** 21.05. – 21.06. (previously Taurus)
		🌿 *Ash - Tree of energy:* 25.05. - 03.06.
Mon 20 -	☾ ●	Pentecost Monday, World Day of Bees
Tue 21	♂ ●	World Day of Cultural Diversity for Dialogue and Development, St. Constantine and Helena Gemini > 21.06.
Wed 22	☿ ●	
Thu 23	♃ ○	full Moon: Flower Moon † Θαργήλια † **B** *Visakha Puja (Vesakh)*
Fri 24	♀ ●	St. Esther
Sat 25	♄ ●	**J** *Lag baOmer (+ 26.05.)*
Sun 26	☉ ●	Trinity Sunday, St. Servatius

~ 65 ~

May Full Moon
Flower Moon

Among the Native American Indigenous the Full Moon in May is called "Flower Moon" because at this time of year everything is in full bloom, with colorful flowers blossoming everywhere.

Witch symbol: Circle

The circle is a symbol of wholeness, completion, perfection, infinity, eternity and the divine spirit. The circle is a symbol of heaven and the destiny of life (wheel of life). It also represents compassion, manifestation. Transformation, longevity, protection, self-development and everything related to the natural cycles of the earth. In magical rituals and practices, the circle protects against evil spirits and demons.

Use the power of the moon:
The waning moon

The waning moon phase (the time from full moon to new moon) again lasts about 14 days. It is **suitable for freeing oneself from negative influences, getting rid of feelings of guilt, vices, bad habits and negative feelings, such as anger, bitterness, jealousy and resentment, as well as ending destructive relationships.** It is the time to look at the negative elements and feelings in our lives in order to overcome them and make room for positivity. The phase of the waning moon is **also suitable for fasting / slimming** and to take time out from everyday life.

Gemini 21.05. – 21.06.

Gemini characteristics are vivacity and youthful appearance, but also duality, falseness and they like to debate.

Good time for magical work, which involves communication, writing, Change of residence and travel have to do.

Planet: Hermes (Mercury) / **Angel:** Raphael / **Olympian spirit:** Ophiel / **Element:** air / **Lucky stones:** magnetic ironstone, opal, agate / **Colors:** blue, light gray, violet, yellow tones / **Lucky day:** Wednesday / **Lucky numbers:** 3, 13, 33 / **Flowers:** forget-me-not, daisy, jasmine / **Metal:** mercury / **Animals:** parrot, monkey, squirrel / **Body parts influenced:** shoulders, arms, hands, fingers, lungs, thymus gland, upper ribs

Gemini in 2024

You will clearly notice that you want to change your life drastically in 2024, even if this involves a change of job, place or faith. You will also be able to enjoy the pleasures of life to the fullest and celebrate your successes extensively. Opportunities for this will be plentiful. However, you will realize that having fun is not everything. It is necessary to be well organized and to put in some work to get things on the right track in your life in order to achieve your goals. You must take responsibility and also fulfill your obligations. Your life philosophy and attitude will change and new ideas, new visions for your future will germinate in you. Your potential will open up a new world for you to work on, but that doesn't mean that every idea you have will be feasible. Always realize that you are very spontaneous and make impulsive decisions. Before you decide on a path, weigh the pros and cons well. It may be that an idea you had last year and for some reason were unable to realize has now matured to the point where it is feasible. It is quite possible that you will be drawn into power games when implementing your plans. Be mindful here and try to be the one in such a situation to break away from the urge to control and create something new together, trusting in the abilities of others. Your strong communication skills will come in handy. Cronos makes you keep a cool head in your actions and proceed in a deliberate and structured manner. Aphrodite helps that the processes of change take place in harmony with your partner and the people close to you.

Both in the summer and in the fall you will take great leaps, all of which will be in preparation for a completely new phase of life. This will be clearly visible from summer 2025 and will last until summer 2033. In 2024, your social environment will also change. Your self-confidence will be boosted by the noticeable progress you have made in realizing your ideas for your future path in life. You will receive recognition in the social and professional environment. But finally, probably the most fundamental proof of your strength and maturity this year is the realization that you are not only prepared to stand up for your freedom, but also to respect the freedom of others.

Gemini: love, family and friends

The sensitive point that mobilized the change process for you was and is in the area of relationships with others. Over the past three years, you realized that many of the relationships that were once very important to you had long since ceased to really work. At the same time, new people you were attracted to entered your life with new views and concepts of life. Passion and romance will be very important in 2024. If you live in a steady partnership, it will be characterized by mutual understanding. You will learn in this year how important a good communication with real listening and responding to each other is for the partnership. You will also find it easier to express your feelings. It pays off now that you have not given up on your love, but have fought for you. 2024 is also a good year for singles among those born under the zodiac sign Gemini. You will have great luck in your search for a partner: Chances are very good that you will find the person who will bring out the best in you and encourage you to rebuild your life from scratch.

Your family appreciates you being there for them like this. However, they are too happy to rely only on you. Make sure you don't let them take advantage of you and make sure the other family members take on their share of responsibilities and obligations.

The year 2024 will bring you some new acquaintances who will greatly enrich your life. You will also receive a lot of advice and active support from them. Concentrate on these new, valuable friendships and distance yourself consistently from all people who only want to take advantage of you.

Gemini: profession and finances

2024 will be a busy year for you professionally. There will also be changes here that have been announced for a long time but have not yet come to fruition due to your uncertainty. But now you are ready to learn and expand your knowledge. You are working hard for your position and your professional progress is causing some envy. Do not let this unsettle you and divert you from your path to success. Concentrate fully on your work.

There will be a large cash inflow at the beginning of the year due to previous investments. In addition, there is a good chance of a salary increase. However, still be careful with unexpected expenses and avoid senseless purchases and investments. It is better to invest in projects with which you can earn money.

Gemini: health

2024 will bring you stable mental and physical health. However, you must be careful not to burn yourself out and waste your energy on pointless things. Avoid stressful situations that endanger your balance.

May / June

CW 22	♊	*Gemini* 21.05. – 21.06.
Mon 27	☾	
Tue 28	♂	† Σκιροφόρια †
Wed 29	☿	
Thu 30	♃	half moon waning, Corpus Christi
Fri 31	♀	Visitation of the Blessed Virgin Mary, St. Petronella
Sat 1	♄	Feast of the goddess Carna, England's witchcraft act of 1563 goes into effect
Sun 2	☉	

Monthly trend June	love	friends, family	profession, money
Aries	☼	☼☼☼☼☼	☼☼☼☼☼
Taurus	☼☼☼☼☼	☼☼	☼
Gemini	☼☼	☼☼	☼☼
Cancer	☼☼☼☼☼	☼☼	☼☼☼☼☼
Leo	☼☼	☼☼☼☼	☼☼
Virgo	☼☼☼☼☼	☼☼	☼
Libra	☼☼☼☼	☼☼☼	☼☼☼☼☼
Scorpio	☼☼	☼☼☼☼☼	☼
Sagittarius	☼☼☼☼☼	☼☼	☼☼☼☼
Capricorn	☼	☼☼☼☼☼	☼☼
Aquarius	☼☼	☼☼	☼☼
Pisces	☼☼☼☼☼	☼☼☼☼☼	☼☼

Goddess Carna

Carna (also called Kore, Ker, Cardea or Carmenta) is the Roman goddess of health, because she is considered the guardian of the "nobler organs" of the human being – the heart (cardiology) and the other vital organs. She is also the goddess of thresholds, door hinges and handles. That is why she is also called the heart and door goddess. She is also the goddess of nutrition and takes care of the physical well-being of people.

$$\Omega \diamondsuit \Omega$$

The number is the essence of all things.
Pythagoras

Pythagoras / Harmony of the Worlds

June

CW 23	♊	**Gemini** 21.05. – 21.06.
		Hornbeam – Tree of perseverance: 04. - 13.06.
Mon 3 +	☾	
Tue 4 -	♂ ☾	J Yom Yerushalayim (+ 05.06.)
Mi 5 +	☿ ☾	World Environment Day
Thu 6	♃ ☉	new moon
Fri 7 +	♀ ☽	
Sat 8	♄ ☽	World Oceans Day
Sun 9 +	☉ ☽	Feast of the goddess Estia

~ 71 ~

Goddess Estia (Hestia)

As the goddess of fire, Estia brings warmth into the house. She is considered the protector of the family and of domestic peace. Estia is the goddess of the family and state hearth, of the hearth and sacrificial fire and one of the 12 Olympian gods until she gave up her place to Dionysus.

Witch symbols: Horned god and Triple moon

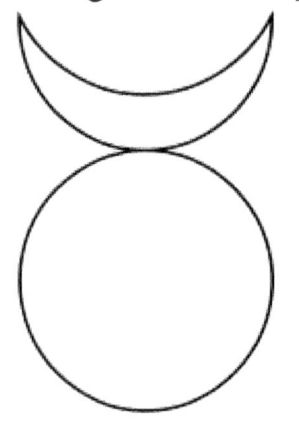

This witch symbol represents the **horned god** and is the counterpart of the triune goddess. The horned god is the god of witchcraft. He is also the god of hunting, nature, human instincts and wild animals.

As a witch sign, it symbolizes masculine energy, the divine masculine. The most common gods represented by this symbol are the Greek god Pan and the Celtic god Cernunnos. The use of this hex sign in rituals helps to gain masculine (fighting) power.

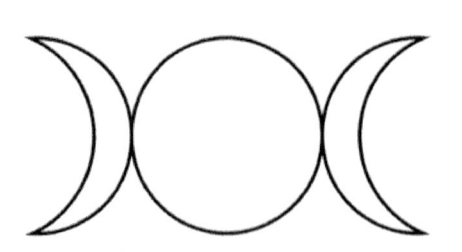

The **triple moon** symbol symbolizes the three phases of the moon with their respective appropriate magical processes: the waxing moon, the waning moon and the full moon. This symbol is also called the triple goddess. Then it represents the three phases of femininity: Virgin, Mother and Old Woman.

June

CW 24	♊	**Gemini** *21.05. – 21.06.*
		🌿 ***Fig Tree - Tree of harmony:** 14. - 23.06.*
Mon 10	☾	St. Margaret
Tue 11	♂	*J Shavuot (until 13.06.)*, St. Barnabas
Wed 12	☿	
Thu 13 +	♃	✝ *Ascension*, 💎 *St. Anthony Feast Day (Sandia Pueblo)* St. Anthony
Fri 14	♀	**half moon waxing**, World Blood Donor Day
Sat 15	♄	St. Veit
Sun 16	☉	*I Feast of the Sacrifice (until 20.06.)*, St. Benno

June

CW 25	♋	**Cancer** 22.06. – 22.07. (previously Gemini)
Mon 17	☾ ●	
Tue 18	♂ ●	
Wed 19	☿ ●	Juneteenth (Liberation of African American United States population from slavery), St. Gervasius
Thu 20 -	♃ ●	World Refugee Day
Fri 21	♀ ●	**Litha**, Summer solstice, Beginning of summer
Sat 22	♄ ○	full moon: Strawberry Moon Cancer > 22.07. † *Saturday of the souls*
Sun 23 +	☉ ●	† *Pentecost*

June Full Moon
Strawberry Moon

In June the wild strawberries ripen in the homeland of the Native American Indigenous. This is where the name "Strawberry Moon" comes from for the Full Moon in June.

Litha 21. June

The summer solstice on June 21 represents the high point, the longest day of the year. **The sun is 0 degrees in Cancer.** Now the days become shorter again and the nights longer. On the day of the summer solstice, the forces of nature have reached their highest level. Goddess Moon can now be fertilized by God Sun. The brave dare to jump over the fire on this sun festival to receive strength, protection, health and purification. The fires are said to have blessing power: The higher they are, the greater the blessing that emanates from them. Wishes made on Litha are said to come true. Incense, lemon, rose and lavender are used. The altar is decorated with summer flowers and fruits. The colors of the feast are yellow and orange. Often there is also a sword on the altar and a mirror to catch the sun and the flames of the fire, respectively. Litha is a good day to bless and protect family and pets in a circle.

Dragon oil and Dragon powder

Dragon oil and also Dragon powder are important and very powerful magical ingredients in witchcraft rituals. The main ingredient is the "Dragon blood". This is a resin obtained from a variety of different plant species. The bright red pigment gives it the name Dragon's blood. However, the products available for purchase today are not exactly the same in composition as those used for magical purposes in earlier times.

Recipe for the dragon powder: about ½ teaspoon each of Sangre de Drago, Daemonorops draco, Dragon blood powder, lime blossom, sage and patchouli.

For the dragon oil, add an additional 3 tablespoons of cannabis or olive oil.

Cancer 22.06. – 22.07.

Cancerians are usually caring, protective, tender and understanding, but also tend to cling to someone and worry constantly.

Good time for magic work
around the family and home life

Planet: Selene (Moon) / **Angel:** Gabriel / **Olympian spirit:** Phul / **Element:** water / **Lucky stones:** pearl, emerald, moonstone and opal / **Colors:** silver, pink, pastel shades / **Lucky day:** Monday / **Lucky numbers:** 2, 12, 72 / **Flowers:** lily, jasmine, gardenia / **Metal:** silver / **Animals:** swan, cat, rabbit, peaceful animals in need of protection / **Body parts influenced:** stomach, diaphragm, chest, lymphatic system, liver, gall bladder

Cancer in 2024

2024 will help you organize and gradually implement the necessary changes by the end of the year. Very important at first is to tackle your family problems and to find answers for the open questions that always lead to contradictions and misunderstandings. Your emotional life is also in turmoil and you don't quite know where you actually belong. 2024 will help you to find more clarity in this matter. The same applies to your professional orientation. You let yourself be strongly influenced and put under pressure by your environment. Often you have tried to adapt to situations you did not choose or did not want to be in this way. In 2024 you will overcome some challenges and put your life in order. You will develop a new strong personality in 2024 and will no longer let yourself be controlled like a puppet.

Stay in control and listen to your needs. Stand by yourself and your desires. This will give you the confidence you need to get through the difficult times. This year is ideal for getting rid of bad habits that hinder your personal and professional growth.

Many things will work in your favor in 2024, and this is mainly due to your hard work, determination, dedication and perseverance. The year starts off calmly at first, but soon the influence of Zeus and Cronos makes itself felt. Especially in your professional life there is a lot to check and correct. 2024 is a turbulent year for you, full of opportunities that you should make the most of. It is a very important year for you and requires careful planning, right decisions as well as a lot of hard work. For the wise, it will open up new avenues and unimagined opportunities, but for the reckless, it will bring many disappointments.
As far as your financial situation is concerned, a stable year awaits you in 2024.

Cancer: love, family and friends

The planetary environment in 2024 will be extremely favorable for love relationships especially in the context of devotion. For those in a partnership, 2024 is an ideal year to further strengthen it. Mutual understanding is important for this. Show your partner that you believe in him/her and stand by him/her in good times and bad. However, if the rifts in the relationship are deep, 2024 is more likely to help you finally end such a partnership and thus say goodbye to burdens you have suffered from for years. In any case, in 2024 you will discard many routines that have made your relationship boring. At the beginning of summer you will be required to make concrete decisions and clarify unclear circumstances and matters.

Singles will also experience many moments of bliss in 2024, either with themselves or because they are at the beginning of a romantic relationship.

After resolving some differences right at the beginning of the year, everything will flow very harmoniously on the family level for most of the year. Uranus continues to help you stand up for your rights. Pay special attention to your family this year and spend enough time with them. Deal with the individual members and try to understand them and your needs in order to be able to support them in the best possible way.

2024 will be a good year for you to meet new people and make friends. Expand your social circle and include people from the past again. You will experience that strangers quickly become so familiar to them that they are almost as important as their family to them.

Cancer: profession and finances

Whereas in 2023 many things rippled along in a relatively undetermined manner, in 2024 we will see concrete, sometimes even radical changes, possibly even shifts in positions within your department or company. This is particularly evident in the period from mid-March to mid-May. Despite the hardships you have experienced, the past year has helped you see many things more clearly, make decisions, and plan for changes in your career field. You need to work hard to ensure that your career takes an upward trend. It is up to you to do the things that you really want and make you happy. Take advantage of all opportunities to work for yourself. Then you will be at your best and leave all competition behind. In business terms, you will make good returns. So if you plan to start a business, 2024 is the best year.

Take a disciplined approach to your finances. Compared to the previous year, your financial situation will continuously improve. Take precautions and invest in projects about which you have informed yourself in detail beforehand and which do not involve a great deal of risk. Perhaps the purchase of a property, which will provide you with future rental income, is a good option for you. In the second half of the year, important contracts may be signed on a professional and/or financial level. Check them very carefully, because there may be dubious aspects hidden in them.

Cancer: health

Your health will be on the upswing again in 2024. However, it is not yet stable and it is important that you take very good care of yourself and, despite all the work and tasks you have to do, always find peace and avoid stress.

June

CW 26	♋	**Cancer** 22.06. – 22.07. 🌿 ***Birch - Tree of light:*** *24.06.* / 🌿 ***Apple tree - Tree of love:*** *25.06. - 04.07.*
Mon 24	☽ ●	St. John's Day, 💎 *St. John Feast Day (Ohkay Owingeh Pueblo)*
Tue 25	♂ ●	
Wed 26	☿ ●	
Thu 27	♃ ●	The Letter of Paul to the Romans
Fri 28	♀ ◐	half moon waning
Sat 29	♄ ☾	St. Peter, St. Paul, 💎 *St. Peter and Paul Feast day*
Sun 30	☉ ☾	† *All Saints Day*

Runes: The Ancient Futhark

By the 5th century, a largely uniform runic script had developed:
the Elder Futhark, consisting of 24 runes.

1. Fe / Fehu (= F)
Rune of fulfillment, wealth (material, ideal, spiritual) possession and prosperity, fertility, energy flow as well as letting go.

2. Ur / Uruz (= U)
Rune of (physical and mental) strength, endurance, courage and untamed wildness, masculinity as well as health.

3. Thorn / Thurisaz (= Q)
Rune of the gateway, the forces of the unconscious, unbridled anger and desire, of doing nothing and being there for self-reflection

4. As / Ansuz (= A)
Rune of controlled, creative and divine power, prophecy and revelation, wisdom, knowledge and reason, and self-acceptance. This rune has a similar meaning to the Greek word "Logos", the spoken word of God.

5. Rad / Raidho / Raido (= R)
This rune means driving, riding or traveling. In a deeper sense, it also stands for the rhythm of life. This rune is also about communication, self-transformation, self-healing and unity.

6. Ken / Kenaz / Kaunaz (= K)
This rune of openness sheds light on our life path, dispels uncertainty and helps to recognize the essential and let go of old inhibiting. It also stands for creativity, new ideas and spiritual enlightenment.

7. Gifu / Gebo (= G)
„Gifu" means dower, gift. This rune symbolically represents the bond of mutual affection according to the principle: "Everything you send into the world comes back to you". Rune of unity, union and partnership.

8. Wynn / Wunju (= W)
Rune of happiness. It is associated with a reward, with joy and satisfaction, a peaceful victory or the achievement of a goal. On the spiritual level, "Wynn" stands for closeness to God and it helps clarity.

9. Hagal / Hagalaz (= H)
"Hagal" means an elemental change. This rune can also symbolize boundaries, interruptions, and delays, and can also herald hardship, illness, or injury. Hagal is a winter rune. Its coldness purifies and heals, but not gently, but radically and consistently.

10. Nyd / Naudhiz / Nauthiz (= N)
Rune of the Norns (goddesses of fate in Germanic mythology). It stands for neediness, hardship or adverse circumstances. But it also includes perseverance and reserves of strength. It brings our shadows before our eyes, helps in the conscious recognition and asks us to let go of all illusions and let our own light become the life force.

11. Is / Isa (= I)
It is the rune of neutrality and means ice. Its surface is smooth and can break easily. So "Is" can signify an obstacle to success and make it clear that plans must be postponed until a more convenient time. "Is" indicates coldness of feeling, but can also take the heat out of an argument and protect against magic. "Is" marks the phase of passivity that precedes rebirth.

12. Ger / Jera (= J)
Rune of good fortune. "Ger" indicates the center of the futhark and means year. It stands for the whole circle of seasons and in particular for the harvest and fertility of autumn. It is a rune of movement, change and development.

13. Eoh / Eihwaz / Eiwaz (= Ä)
"Eoh" means yew (tree of life). The yew is closely associated with death, but also with rebirth, new beginnings. This rune indicates a blockage on our path, but it can also be useful. In the calm lies the power, patience is advisable.

14. Peorth / Peord / Perthro (= P)
"Peorth" stands for the cauldron of Cerridwen, who dips fallen warriors into the cauldron so that they can be reborn. This rune is a symbol of fate, from which one should make the best. It announces the revelation of a secret. And it shows that deep, inner, transforming forces are at work.

15. Eolx / Algiz (= Z)
It is a rune with great protective power, symbolizing the pursuit of the divine. "Eolx" also applies to success and perseverance in hunting, a quest or any other endeavor. This rune is also about the control of emotions. "Eolx" means moose: as an animal of the swamp and marshland, it brings light and clarity to diffuse matters.

16. Sigel / Sowilo / Sowelo (= S)
"Sigel" is known as a symbol of victory. But this rune can also mean the power of an attack. It carries the power of the sun and represents a clear view, the victory of light over darkness. "Sigel" is the rune of fulfillment, profit and prosperity, as well as farewell to the past.

17. Tyr / Tiwaz / Teiwaz (= T)
The rune "Tyr" is directly connected with Tyr (God of war) and his qualities. It symbolizes decisiveness, the achievement of goals and male sexuality. It is also about character building and the necessary look inside, the descent to the foundations of our lives.

18. Beorc / Berkana (= B)
"Beorc" corresponds to the qualities of Artemis, the Greek goddess of the hunt, the forest and the moon, birth, and the guardian of women and children. This rune involves renewal, revitalization, purification, healing, recovery. It is the rune of family and home, represents pleasurable sexuality, fertility, birth. It leads to flowering and maturity.

19. Ehwaz (= E)
"Ehwaz" means horse. Because of their speed, strength and beauty, they were more than just a means of transportation. It symbolizes real and spiritual locomotion (development) as a sacred animal. "Ehwaz" is a rune of transition and movement. It stands for measured change, progress, journey. It also symbolizes partnership, trust, loyalty and faithfulness.

20. Man / Mannaz (= M)
This rune represents the common human nature that everyone has within them. It also addresses creativity, intelligence, communication and thoughtful planning for the future. It also encourages not to capitulate to challenges, as well as to break old habits if they are inhibiting.

21. Lagu / Laguz (= L)
"Lagu" means water, vital element and at the same time danger. This rune contains movement, change and uncontrollable forces. It also stands for the infatuation of the senses through sexuality, emotions, unconscious and intuition.

22. Ing / Inguz (= Ö)
The main meaning of the rune Ing is completion, the certainty that everything will reach its conclusion. Ing was a fertility god with the same qualities as Frey. Thus, this rune stands for healthy, natural sexuality, strong and loving family cohesion and a safe home. It also symbolizes spiritual development.

23. Dag / Dagaz (= D)
"Dag" means day and is a symbol of (divine) light and life in the Nordic countries with their long nights and winters. Therefore, the rune "Dag" indicates brightness, growth, progress, development and sometimes fundamental change. This rune heralds a major breakthrough and thrust in the process of self-transformation, a complete transformation in attitude.

24. Odal / Othala / Othila (= O)
This last rune of the Futhark means goal, fatherland or homeland, possession, secured prosperity or inheritance. This can also include character traits that one has inherited from grandparents and will still pass on to grandchildren. "Odal" embodies the sum of all that one has accumulated and experienced in life. This rune also means the strength of a united family.

Altes Futhark

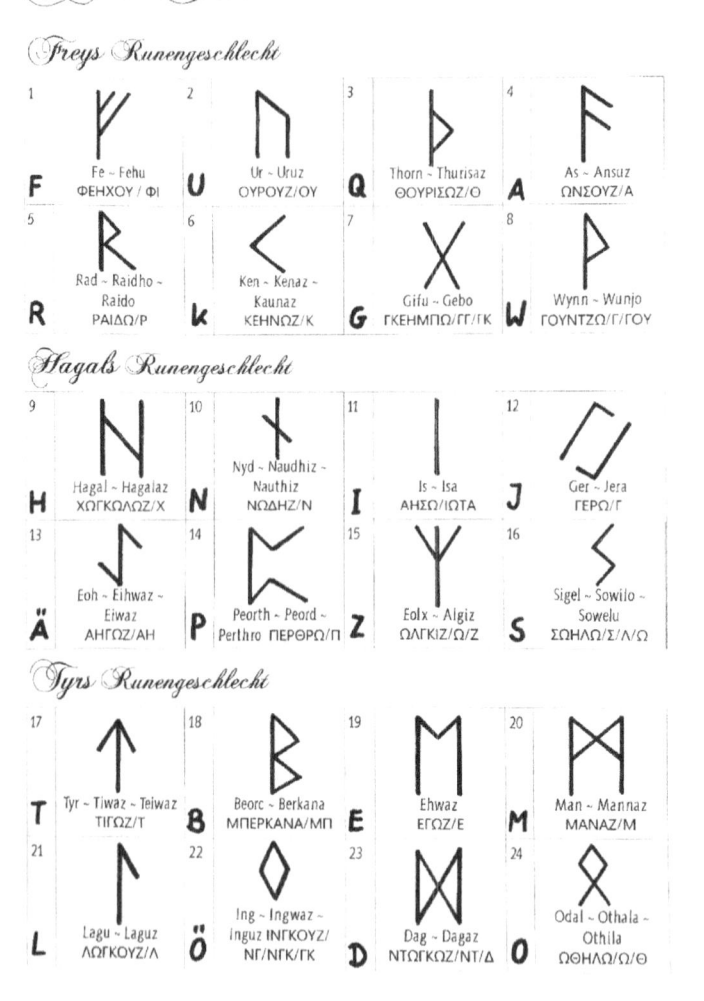

Freys Runengeschlecht

1	ᚠ	Fe ~ Fehu	F — ΦΕΗΧΟΥ / ΦΙ
2	ᚢ	Ur ~ Uruz	U — ΟΥΡΟΥΖ/ΟΥ
3	ᚦ	Thorn ~ Thurisaz	Q — ΘΟΥΡΙΣΩΖ/Ο
4	ᚨ	As ~ Ansuz	A — ΩΝΣΟΥΖ/Α
5	ᚱ	Rad ~ Raidho ~ Raido	R — ΡΑΙΔΩ/Ρ
6	ᚲ	Ken ~ Kenaz ~ Kaunaz	k — ΚΕΗΝΩΖ/Κ
7	ᚷ	Gifu ~ Gebo	G — ΓΚΕΗΜΠΩ/ΓΓ/ΓΚ
8	ᚹ	Wynn ~ Wunjo	W — ΓΟΥΝΤΖΩ/Γ/ΓΟΥ

Hagals Runengeschlecht

#	Rune	Name	Transliteration
9	ᚺ	Hagal ~ Hagalaz	H — ΧΩΓΚΩΛΩΖ/Χ
10	ᚾ	Nyd ~ Naudhiz ~ Nauthiz	N — ΝΩΔΗΖ/Ν
11	ᛁ	Is ~ Isa	I — ΑΗΣΩ/ΙΩΤΑ
12	ᛃ	Ger ~ Jera	J — ΓΕΡΩ/Γ
13	ᛇ	Eoh ~ Eihwaz ~ Eiwaz	Ä — ΑΗΓΩΖ/ΑΗ
14	ᛈ	Peorth ~ Peord ~ Perthro	P — ΠΕΡΘΡΩ/Π
15	ᛉ	Eolx ~ Algiz	Z — ΩΛΓΚΙΖ/Ω/Ζ
16	ᛋ	Sigel ~ Sowilo ~ Sowelu	S — ΣΩΗΛΩ/Σ/Λ/Ω

Tyrs Runengeschlecht

#	Rune	Name	Transliteration
17	ᛏ	Tyr ~ Tiwaz ~ Teiwaz	T — ΤΙΓΩΖ/Τ
18	ᛒ	Beorc ~ Berkana	B — ΜΠΕΡΚΑΝΑ/ΜΠ
19	ᛖ	Ehwaz	E — ΕΓΩΖ/Ε
20	ᛗ	Man ~ Mannaz	M — ΜΑΝΑΖ/Μ
21	ᛚ	Lagu ~ Laguz	L — ΛΩΓΚΟΥΖ/Λ
22	ᛜ	Ing ~ Ingwaz ~ Inguz	Ö — ΙΝΓΚΟΥΖ/ΝΓ/ΝΓΚ/ΓΚ
23	ᛞ	Dag ~ Dagaz	D — ΝΤΩΓΚΩΖ/ΝΤ/Δ
24	ᛟ	Odal ~ Othala ~ Othila	O — ΩΘΗΛΩ/Ω/Θ

In the great Witchbook – the basic work of witchcraft with over 270 pages – there is also a very detailed chapter about the runes. There, for example, the physical, mental, spiritual and magical effect of each rune is described.

July

CW 27	♋	**Cancer** 22.06. – 22.07.
		Fir – Tree of foresight: 05. - 14.07.
Mon 1	☽	
Tue 2 +	♂	
Wed 3	☿	Feast of the goddess Cerridwen
Thu 4	♃	Ortisei
Fri 5 -	♀	
Sat 6 +	♄	new moon, *I Islamic New Year (+ 07.07.)*
Sun 7	☉	

Monthly trend July	love	friends, family	profession, money
Aries	☼☼	☼☼☼☼☼	☼☼☼☼
Taurus	☼☼☼☼☼☼	☼☼☼	☼☼☼☼☼☼
Gemini	☼☼	☼☼☼☼☼	☼☼
Cancer	☼☼☼☼☼☼	☼☼	☼☼☼
Leo	☼☼	☼	☼☼
Virgo	☼☼☼☼☼☼	☼☼☼☼	☼☼
Libra	☼☼	☼☼	☼☼
Scorpio	☼☼☼	☼	☼☼☼
Sagittarius	☼☼☼☼☼☼	☼☼☼☼	☼☼☼☼☼
Capricorn	☼☼☼☼☼☼	☼☼	☼☼
Aquarius	☼☼	☼☼☼☼☼	☼☼
Pisces	☼☼☼☼☼☼	☼☼	☼☼☼

Goddess Cerridwen

03. July is the feast day of the goddess Cerridwen, the Celtic-Welsh goddess of the earth, harvest, grain and fertility. She is the goddess of the moon and protector of regeneration, of inspiration, herbs, science, poetry, spells and wisdom, goddess of death and rebirth. Cerridwen is the goddess with the cauldron in which the primordial soup simmers. While the ingredients are mixed and transformed by the heat, new thoughts are created while stirring. The cauldron symbolizes the belly of the goddess, from which all life comes and into which it also returns.

Witch symbol: Hexagram

The Hexagram is a widespread symbol in occultism and witchcraft, and it is considered the sign of the ever-present Freemasons. The Hexagram, also known as the "Star of David", represents the coexistence of good and evil, or in other words, there can be no good without the involvement of evil.

Since the Hexagram consists of two inverted triangles joined into one, this symbol symbolizes the unity and oneness of opposites. It can refer to the unity of man and woman, light and darkness, and in alchemy to the seemingly impossible union of fire and water, earth and air. The upper triangle of the Hexagram with the angle pointing upward symbolizes the spiritual world, while the lower triangle, upside down, represents earthly life. The Hexagram represents the seven ancient planets: Cronos (Saturn), Zeus (Jupiter), Ares (Mars), Aphrodite (Venus), Hermes (Mercury), Helios (Sun) and Selene (Moon). Sun and Moon were also considered as planets in the past. Therefore, the Hexagram is often used in cosmic rituals. But the Hexagram is also considered an evil goth symbol because it has 6 points and 6 sides, just like the infamous number 666.

July

CW 28	♋	**Cancer** 22.06. – 22.07.
Mon 8	☾ ☽	St. Kilian
Tue 9	♂ ☽	
Wed 10 +	☿ ☽	Seven Brothers Day (Felicitas and her sons)
Thu 11	♃ ☽	
Fri 12	♀ ☽	† Saint Paisios of Mount Athos
Sat 13 +	♄ ☽	
Sun 14	☉ ☽	half moon waxing 💎 St. Bonaventure Feast Day (Cochiti Pueblo)

Sokushinbutsu: Mummified Monks

In the mountain world of Japan, a religion called **Shugendō** arose in the 7th century, in which strict asceticism is practiced until today. This special religion is a syncretism, meaning a mixed form, of Vajrayana Buddhism, Shintoism and Taoism. One of these practices was **Sokushinbutsu**, which means to follow the mountain disciplines in order to achieve the nature of Buddha in one's own body. This practice was perfected over time, **especially in the "Three Mountains of Dewa" region of Japan**, which is the area of Haguro, Gassan and Yudono mountains. These mountains are sacred in the Shugendō tradition until today, and in the valleys and mountain ranges of this area monks still live in ascetic strictness.

The mystical Vairocana and Vajraśekhara tantras are expressed in the two main Mandalas of Shingon, the **Mandala of the "Two Worlds": the Mandala of the "Mother's Womb Kingdom" and the Mandala of the "Diamond Kingdom"**. These two Mandalas are seen as a compact expression of the entirety of the Dharma and **are the foundation of Buddhism**. In Shingon temples, these two Mandalas are always placed on each side of the central altar. The Susiddhikara Sūtra is for the most part a compendium of rituals. Tantric Buddhism is concerned with the rituals and meditative practices that lead to enlightenment. In medieval Japan, this tradition developed a **process for Sokushinbutsu, which a monk completed over about 3,000 days**. It involved a **strict diet called Mokujiki (literally "eating a tree")**. The diet eliminated all grains and was based on pine needles, resins and seeds found in the mountains that would eliminate all fat in the body. **Fasting and meditation would lead to the sacred level.**

The monks died in a condition of Jhana (meditation) while chanting the Nenbutsu (a mantra about Buddha), and **their bodies naturally became mummies** with their skin and teeth intact **without the use of synthetic conservation methods**. Especially in northern Japan, many centuries-old Buddhist Sokushinbutsu mummies have been found, buried in stupas and mountain caves. These are highly revered by people of the Buddhist faith.

Luang Pho Daeng was a Thai Buddhist monk who died during meditation in 1973 and was preserved in such a mummified way. Luang was born in Thailand in 1894. In his twenties, he was not yet ready for his childhood dream of becoming a monk. So he decided to marry first and raised six children with his wife. After all his children were grown up, Luang, who was now 50 years old, finally decided to become a Buddhist monk. He was shortly an abbot in a temple in southern Thailand, but then moved to Wat Khunaram near his parents' home. He practiced a life of Sokushinbutsu, that previously described form of self-mummification.

Luang died during meditation in 1973, and **his mummified body can be seen at Wat Khunaram (temple) on the island of Ko Samui in Thailand's Surat Thani province**. The mummy is characterized by wearing sunglasses placed by groundskeepers to cover its decomposed eye sockets, making it less frightening to look at. Native Gecko birds use its body as a nesting site, laying eggs under the skin.

July

CW 29	♋	**Cancer** 22.06. – 22.07.
		🌿 **Elm - Tree of awakening:** 15. - 25.07.
Mon 15	☾	† Holy Martyr Cyricus and his mother Julitta
Tue 16	♂	I Ashura (+ 17.07.) † Ἑκατομβαιών †
Wed 17	☿	† Holy Great Martyr Marina, St. Alexius
Thu 18 +	♃	
Fri 19 -	♀	St. Vincent
Sat 20	♄	† Glorious prophet Elias (Elijah)
Sun 21	☉	full moon: Buck Moon

~ 87 ~

July Full Moon

Buck Moon

Among the Native American Indigenous the Full Moon in July
is called the "Buck Moon" because this is the time
when deer roam the forests of North America.
Every year in midsummer, the buck grows new antlers.
This is also where the "Buck Moon" has its roots.

Witch symbol: Anch

This ancient Egyptian symbol is also called the key of life. It is a symbol of the universe, (eternal) life, immortality and rebirth. It is a combination of the male and female symbols for Osiris and Isis and thus expresses in the union of the two the common creative power of heaven and earth.

The Anch sign symbolizes the rising sun along with the balance of feminine and masculine energies. It is a protective symbol and it can also be used to mark the boundaries of sacred spaces. The ancient Egyptian gods are often depicted holding the key of life in one hand with arms folded in front of the chest. The Anch symbol corresponds to the ancient astrological sign of Aphrodite.

$\Omega \diamondsuit \Omega$

*If you can't have a faithful friend,
be your own friend.*

Pythagoras

July

CW 30	♌	**Leo 23.07. – 23.08.** (previously Cancer)
		🌿 **Cypress – Tree of eternity:** 26.07. - 04.08.
Mon 22	☾ ●	J *Shiva Assar beTammus (+ 23.07.)*, St. Maria Magdalena
Tue 23	♂ ●	St. Apollinaris **Leo > 23.08.**
Wed 24	☿ ●	
Thu 25	♃ ●	💎 *Santiago Feast Day (Taos Pueblo)*, St. Jakobus
Fri 26	♀ ●	St. Anna
Sat 27 -	♄ ●	St. Panteleimon
Sun 28	☉ ☽	half moon waning † Κρόνια - Παναθήναια †
		† St. Irene Chrysovalantou

Magic plants

Alant ~ *Inula helenium:* male / Hermes / air
Forces: love, protection, strength, encouragement, clairvoyance, meditation.

Birch ~ *Betula alba:* female / Aphrodite / water
Forces: protection, purification (exorcism), love

Boswellia / Incense resin ~ *Boswellia Sacra:* male / Helios / fire
Forces: protection, blessing, spirituality

Damiana ~ *Turnera aphrodisia:* male / Ares / fire
Forces: love, sensuality, visions

Dandelion ~ *Taraxacum officinale:* male / Zeus / air
Forces: clairvoyance, wish fulfillment, cleansing, spirit summoning

Hawthorn ~ *Crataegus oxyacantha:* male / Ares (Mars) / fire
Forces: defense, protection, chastity, potency, fertility

Hazelnut ~ *Corylus avellana:* male / Aphrodite / water
Forces: fertility, wishes, luck, protection, power, divination, prophecy, wisdom

Lavender ~ *Lavendula angustifolia:* masculine / Hermes / air
Forces: purification, protection, sleep, love, peace, joy

Lilac ~ *Syringa vulgaris:* female / Aphrodite / water
Forces: fertility, love, protection

Palo Santo ~ *Bursera graveolens:* male / Hermes / air
Forces: luck, blessing, attraction, success, health, balance, purification

Rosemary ~ *Rosmarinus officinalis:* male / Helios / fire
Forces: healing, purification, exorcism, sleep, protection, love, passion

Sage ~ *Salvia officinalis:* male / Zeus / air
Forces: purification, longevity, wisdom, clarity, protection, wish fulfillment, health

Sweet grass ~ *Hierochloe odorata:* female / Aphrodite / water
Forces: attract good spirits, love, peace, harmony, blessing

Willow ~ *Salix alba:* female / Selene / water
Forces: healing, protection, growth, love

Wormwood ~ *Artemisia absinthium:* male / Ares (Mars) / fire
Forces: protection, health, divination / prophecy, love, sensuality

Yerba Santa ~ *Eriodictycon glutinosum:* male / Ares / fire
Forces: healing, protection, self-confidence, drive

Leo 23.07. – 23.08.

The Leo is a leader, an organizational talent, enthusiastic, creative and generous, but can also be tyrannical and very rigid in his views.

**Good time for magic work
on the topics of power, authority, courage,
fertility and birth**

Planet: Helios (Sun) / **Angel:** Michael / **Olympian spirit:** Och / **Element:** fire / **Lucky Stones:** ruby, diamond / **Colors:** yellow, orange, red, gold / **Lucky day:** Sunday / **Lucky numbers:** 1, 81, 91 / **Flowers:** sunflower, golden rain / **Metal:** gold / **Animals:** panther, cat, canary, thoroughbred horse, eagle / **Body parts influenced:** heart, aorta, back, spine

Leo in 2024

2024 will bring you prosperity and abundance and thanks to your tireless work everything will change for the better. By remaining diligent, you will master the year with all its ups and downs brilliantly. Zeus will not only strengthen you, but will make you really enthusiastic about many things. But be careful with all your enthusiasm and don't overdo it. You cannot dance on all weddings and have to decide. This applies to your ideas and projects as well as to your many wishes. Keep an eye on your finances here and don't go overboard.

You will have to overcome some challenges at work in 2024. However, you will ultimately emerge victorious. Conventional strategies will inhibit you, however. Think and act creatively and innovatively. It is important that you consistently stay away from any people who are jealous of you and your career. The second half of the year will offer you much more than you dare hope. September and October are the best months to improve the climate in your professional environment and also to advance or intensify partnerships.

Avoid falling into the traps of false friends. Listen to your heart and your gut feeling in everything you do. Then you will make the right decisions. Be more generous to those around you this year and help make the world a better place through community service. Take more responsibility this year and put your energy into the right things. Try to be more true to yourself and take off the masks you wear for show and to protect yourself from others. Redesign your free time and make new contacts. Possibly, for you as a person with team spirit, club life or involvement in groups of like-minded people is something for you.

Leo: love, family and friends

The year 2024 brings some trials in the area of love for those born under the zodiac sign Leo. There may be separations or commitments that put a strain on your relationship. But in any case, the desire for a lasting, stable partnership matures in you and for this you are also ready to do and also to change a lot.

Among these changes that will be good for your partnership is better communication with your partner. Make an effort to save your relationship if it is important to you. However, if you notice that the love has gone out, then do not wait any longer, but separate and thus free yourself from emotional burden.

On a family level, there will be harmony and tranquility for you in 2024. Any differences you have with your loved ones will be resolved diplomatically and fairly. This behavior will be appreciated by family members and you will receive support from them in what you want to achieve in your life.

In your social environment you need to make some changes, because you will find that you are surrounded by false friends. Detach yourself from them or they will continue to abuse your trust and deceive you.

Leo: profession and finances

2024 is favorable for spreading your wings in new directions, whether it's new business deals or a trip abroad. At the beginning of the year, you will probably have to face some professional challenges, including the fact that your colleagues at work are jealous of your success. So be careful not to make any mistakes. Showcase your talents and make the most of your skills. But avoid remaining a lone wolf or becoming one. True leadership quality is characterized by the fact that you manage to inspire your colleagues about the work or your joint project, so that they also apply themselves in the best possible way and contribute to the success. In addition, you may learn new ways of working yourself. As the year progresses, professional things will improve for you and you may even expect a promotion and a more challenging task. 2024 is also a very good year for you to start your own business.

For most of the year you will have financial liquidity, but that doesn't mean you can rest. Consistently look for new sources of income so that you can continue to live without financial worries. Be creative in choosing investment options and be brave enough to take advantage of the opportunities offered to you. This may involve the purchase and sale of real estate, but also income from rentals or alimony payments due to you after the separation from your partner for the care of the joint child/children.

Leo: health

You'll be paying close attention to your physical condition, habits, diet and exercise in 2024, especially during the period from March to June. Stress at work and a packed daily routine will take their toll, although at least you won't have to worry much about your health for most of the year. However, you will be concerned about the health of some people close to you. Here, make sure they get all the medical care they need. Nevertheless, do not forget to take care of your own well-being continuously as well.

July / August

CW 31	♌	**Leo** *23.07. – 23.08.*
Mon 29	☽ ☾	St. Olav, St. Beate, St. Lucilla, St. Ladislaus, St. Flora
Tue 30 +	♂ ☾	World Day Against Human Trafficking
Wed 31	☿ ☾	St. Ignatius
Thu 1	♃ ☾	**Lughnasadh / Lammas**, mid-summer, ✝ *The Holy Seven Maccabees Children,* *Salome (their mother) and Eleazar (their teacher)*
Fri 2 -	♀ ☾	♦ *Persingula Feast Day (Jemez Pueblo)* ✝ Συνοίκια ✝
Sat 3	♄ ☾	
Sun 4	☉ ○	**new moon**, ♦ *St. Dominic Feast Day (Santo Domingo Pueblo)*

Monthly trend August	love	friends, family	profession, money
Aries	☼	☼☼☼☼☼	☼☼☼☼☼
Taurus	☼☼☼☼☼	☼☼	☼☼☼☼☼
Gemini	☼☼	☼☼☼☼☼	☼☼
Cancer	☼☼☼☼☼	☼☼	☼☼☼
Leo	☼☼☼☼	☼☼☼☼	☼☼☼☼
Virgo	☼☼☼	☼☼	☼☼☼☼☼
Libra	☼☼☼	☼☼☼☼	☼☼☼
Scorpio	☼☼☼☼☼	☼☼☼☼☼	☼☼☼☼☼
Sagittarius	☼☼☼	☼☼	☼☼
Capricorn	☼☼☼☼☼	☼☼☼☼☼	☼☼☼☼☼
Aquarius	☼☼☼	☼☼☼☼☼	☼
Pisces	☼☼☼	☼☼	☼☼☼☼☼

Lughnasadh / Lammas 01. *August*

The days are getting shorter, the sun is losing its power. Goddess Moon is sad because her partner is slowly coming to his end. But there is also a feeling of happiness in her, because she carries the fruit of her love. On 01. August, according to Celtic custom, the first of three harvest festivals was celebrated: "Lughnasadh". Among the ancient Saxons in England, the day is called "Lammas Day".

Bread baked from the fresh wheat was sacrificed in thanksgiving for the harvest. With the expansion of the Christian religion, Lugh, the Druid god of wisdom, became Lucifer. It is said that he was defeated by the archangel Michael on 1. August and plunged into hell with thunder and lightning. The fact that August often begins with thunderstorms has been equated with the raging of the devil. In the past, people did not start anything new on this day, did not travel, did not get married, did not put on a new piece of clothing.

It is traditional on Lughnasadh to plant some seeds in pots from all the fruits eaten on this day and then to take care of the resulting plantlets with devotion, because they symbolize our relationship with God and the Goddess. A traditional food at Lammas is a homemade bread made of blueberries, corn, apples and grains. The altar is decorated with cornflowers, woven wheat wreaths, corn stalks and sunflowers. Incense is made with sandalwood, rose and aloe. Colors: red, orange.

August

CW 32	♌	**Leo** *23.07. – 23.08.* 🌿 ***Poplar - Tree of self-knowledge:*** *05. - 13.08.*
Mon 5 +	☾	† *Pre-feast of the Transfiguration of our Lord and Savior Jesus Christ*
	🌘	
Tue 6 +	♂	† *Feast of the Transfiguration of Jesus Christ*
	🌘	
Wed 7 +	☿	† *Closing celebration of the Transfiguration of Jesus Christ*, St. Afra (Mary Snow)
	🌘	
Thu 8	♃	St. Dominikus
	🌘	
Fri 9	♀	💎 San Lorenzo Mass (Picuris Pueblo) / Anniversary of the Pueblo Revolt of 1680, International Day of Indigenous Peoples
	🌘	
Sat 10 +	♄	St. Lawrence's Day 💎 San Lorenzo Feast Day (Picuris Pueblo)
	🌘	
Sun 11	☉	
	🌘	

Witch symbol: Cross

It symbolizes the four points of the horizon. The simple equal-sided and upright cross is one of the oldest forms of the cross. It also symbolizes the relationship of God to the human being (vertical axis) and of the human being to his fellows and the world (horizontal axis). The existence of the cross as a symbol goes back to the depths of the ancient world. The cross had a deeper symbolic meaning among the pre-Christian pagan peoples: for the Egyptians it meant the future life. For the ancient Greeks it was a sacred symbol of the Olympian god Zeus. The Romans used it as an instrument of execution. It was a symbol of oppression and punishment, a symbol of the curse. Jesus Christ, who died on the cross, sanctified it. From this time on, the cross was venerated by Christians and considered a sign of redemption and grace, a symbol of Jesus Christ's martyrdom and resurrection.

The candle flame and what it shows us

If air currents do not influence the burning of the candle, it is possible to draw conclusions about the fulfillment or non-fulfillment of the magical wish from the shape and size of the flame and its color.

Blue flame: The request or wish has been received. **White flame:** The higher beings rush to help. **Yellow flame:** The wish was either formulated incomprehensibly. There was a lack of concentration on the goal during the ritual, or the request was rejected. **Bright red flame:** The wish was approved immediately. **Rainbow-colored flame:** This is a very strong omen and a sign of having created a suitable and harmonious energy field for the magical work. **Golden flame:** The golden flame is a very important omen, especially when invoking the angels. In any case, the magical work was perceived by a very significant spiritual being. But beware: Evil creatures may try to deceive you and turn into angels of light. **Normal great flame:** The wish comes true in a slow process. **Great flame:** The wish is supported and carried forward by positive vibrations and etheric forces. **Small flame:** The wish has not been accepted. **Extinguishing flame:** If the flame goes out, then your magical work has not been granted permission. The dying flame can also be a sign of the presence of a creature that wants to disrupt or prevent the ritual. **Hissing flame:** If the candle flame hisses, it is usually an alarm sign and can alert you to impending changes and challenges, or warn you of accidents, dangers, enemies, or the like. The hissing can also alert you to energies in the environment that you have not noticed before. Try to focus on them and if you sense they are negative, block them out. If they are positive, you can invite them to assist you in your magical work.

August

CW 33	♌	**Leo** *23.07. – 23.08.*
		🌿 ***Cedar - Tree of mystery: 14. - 23.08.***
Mon 12	☾	half moon waxing, **J** *Tischa beAv (+ 13.08.)*, 💎 *Santa Clara Feast Day (Santa Clara Pueblo)*, International Youth Day
Tue 13 -	♂	St. Hippolytus, St. Kassian
Wed 14 +	☿	
Thu 15 +	♃	Assumption of the Virgin Mary, ☦ *Dormition of the Most Holy Lady, the Theotokos and Ever Virgin Mary –* 💎 *Is also celebrated by the Zia Pueblo*
Fri 16	♀	St. Rochus · † Μεταγείτνια †
Sat 17	♄	
Sun 18	☉	**J** *Tu B'Av (+ 19.08.)*, St. Agapitus

~ 97 ~

Medicinal plants have the most powerful effect, when you harvest according to the moon

Herbs for drying are best collected during the waning moon. Also dig up roots in the waning moon phase or even directly at new moon. Important: In no case expose to sunlight! Ideal for this are the hours before sunrise or the late evening hours. **Harvest leaves when the moon is waxing.** Exception: Nettle should be harvested when the moon is waning. **Flowers are best picked at full moon or waxing moon, and medicinal herbs are best picked directly at full moon,** as their potency is strongest then. However, **the time of the waning moon is more suitable for drying the flowers,** as they dry faster then. **Harvest fruits and seeds** for immediate use during the **waxing moon.** For **drying**, however, the **waning moon** is more suitable.

Oil extract from flowers and herbs – this is how it's done:

Fill a jar about two-thirds with flowers and / or herbs and pour a good oil. Then heat the filled jar in a water bath and simmer for about 15 minutes, then slowly cool. Put the jar in a warm place and wait for 1 to 3 days. Shake the jar from time to time. If you prefer to use the power of the sun, put the jar in a sunny place. It may take 14 days for the flowers/herbs and oil to combine. You can tell when the oil is "ripe" by the change in color. For pouring, you need a second jar and a coffee filter. This is placed over the second jar so that the rim protrudes and holds the filter in place. Then pour the flower-herb oil into the filter. It will begin to drip into the second jar and it may take a few hours to drain completely.
Pour the oil into a dark bottle and label it with the contents and date.

$$\Omega \diamondsuit \Omega$$

Do nothing,
which you know nothing about,
but let yourself be taught
as much as necessary.
This is how you will
most pleasant life spend.

Pythagoras

August

CW 34	♍	**Virgo** 24.08. – 22.09. (previously Leo)
		🌿 **Pine - Tree of patience:** 24.08. - 02.09.
Mon 19	☾ ●	full moon: Sturgeon Moon, World Humanitarian Day
Tue 20	♂ ●	St. Bernard
Wed 21	☿ ●	† The Holy Apostle Thaddaeus
Thu 22	♃ ●	
Fri 23	♀ ●	
Sat 24	♄ ●	Virgo > 22.09.
Sun 25	☉ ●	† Return of the Body of the Glorious Apostle Bartholomew

August Full Moon
Sturgeon Moon

The name "Sturgeon Moon", which the Native American Indigenous
gave to the Full Moon in August, is based on the sturgeon.
This fish could be caught particularly often in August.

Central theme	Chakra	Way to happiness
connectedness with the universe / gateway to the higher self, spiritual power, spirituality, religiosity, knowledge, inner vision	*Crown* Sahasrara (white, purple, gold)	Think less, feel more
self-awareness, creative energy, intuition, spiritual insight, power of imagination, connection to the incarnated soul	*Forehead* Ajna (blue)	Doubt less, smile more
communication, ego-consciousness, ability to learn and concentrate, rational thinking, individuality	*Throat* Vishuddha (turquoise)	Speech less, hear more
love, warmth of feeling, self-esteem, artistic expression, tolerance, forgiveness	*Heart* Anahata (green)	Judgments less, accept more
ego-feeling, emotionality, compassion, empathy, desire, assertiveness, spontaneity	*Solarplexus* Manipura (yellow)	Observe less, make more
body awareness, vitality, healing energy, procreative power / fertility, enthusiasm, female energy	*Sacral* Svadhisthana (orange)	Complain less, guess more
vitality, self-preservation, endurance, rhythm, closeness to earth and nature, basic trust, perseverance	*Root* Muladhara (red)	Fear less, love more

Virgo 24.08. – 22.09.

Those born under the sign of Virgo think analytically and soberly. They are Health-conscious, practical, talkative and modest. They nag, gossip and are supercritical.

Good time for magic work, that affects all intellectual subjects, but also health, nutrition (diets) and leisure activities

Planet: Hermes (Mercury) / **Angel:** Raphael / **Olympian spirit:** Ophiel / **Element:** earth / **Lucky stones:** sapphire, emerald, topaz / **Colors:** white, yellow, green and earthy tones / **Lucky day:** Wednesday / **Lucky numbers:** 3, 23, 33 / **Flowers:** verbena, aster and hyacinth / **Metal:** mercury / **Animals:** dogs, small pets and swallows / **Body parts influenced:** large intestine, small intestine, pancreas, nerves and spleen

Virgo in 2024

2024 will be a year full of responsibilities and obligations for you. And yet it will also be a year in which you will do and experience many fantastic things. Things will happen that will exceed your expectations. Especially love will play an essential role in your daily life and you will be able to realize your dreams on an emotional level. You will achieve with ease everything you want for your love life. In fact, you will also have the chance to revive relationships with past loves. You will enjoy the periods of rest in 2024 intensely and draw strength from travel, relaxing walks or bike rides in nature and good conversations with friends. Take advantage of the opportunities available to you to achieve your goals. Try to see things from their positive side and you will experience that the universe becomes your ally. Free yourself from any negativity in your life that could prevent you from your personal development and from realizing your life goals. Be kind, helpful and compassionate to those close to you, even if it is sometimes difficult for you because they are sometimes quite demanding and feel sorry for themselves. You will learn important life lessons from them. Move forward. Leave the past behind, make peace with it and let go of negative experiences.

At the beginning of 2024 you can save enough money and autumn is a good time for investments to increase income. Financially, you will have a very productive year and your investments will prove profitable. April will be quite a positive and fruitful month in the field of professional life, especially in terms of teamwork. And also your family environment will be very pleasant for you from April, giving you support and strength for everyday life.

Virgo: love, family and friends

In love relationships you tend to be idealistic. In 2024 it is necessary to be realistic as well and not build castles in the air. In 2024, both Aphrodite and Ares will create aspects in your favor, so your love life will be on the right track. With a bit of commitment and good will, you will find right ways to communicate well with each other in your partnership and avoid conflicting feelings. In fact, you will also have a chance to revive relationships with past loves. 2024 is an excellent year for you to expand and intensify such relationships.

Many Virgo singles will enter into new relationships this year, which will face some challenges, at least in the early days, due to ideological differences.

2024 is ideal to plan changes in your personal life and take time for yourself. Give more attention and time to your family members, as many misunderstandings can arise because you are out of sync with your loved ones.

Your social life will improve greatly, because you will consciously bring people into your life in 2024 with whom you are on the same wavelength, and soon friendships will develop on which you can rely one hundred percent.

Virgo: profession and finances

At the beginning of the year, you lack the motivation to develop professionally and are even on the verge of giving up. Hang in there and grit your teeth. Focus on the positive things in your job and find new ways to motivate yourself and move forward. From April onwards, you will notice how your professional life suddenly takes on new momentum and how you enjoy working productively in a team again. It's up to you to take charge of your career and do what's right for you. Get inspiration and motivation from the people around you and maybe even dare to take the step into self-employment. 2024 is a good year for it. You should pay attention in August. Check carefully beforehand what you sign and do not make any hasty decisions.

You enjoy a steady flow of funds throughout the year, so you don't have to worry. The income comes as you want and need it. Especially at the beginning of the year in the period from 01. January to 20. February, luck is on your side with your finances. Use this period for investments, possibly also for real estate purchases, with which you profit later through rental income. Create also clear conditions and settle your debts and check your expenses for example for insurance regarding optimization. Zeus will help you find a clear path that will also give you long-term financial stability.

Virgo: health

Your energy will be at a very high level. Do what is necessary to ensure that your health remains excellent. You are already doing a lot through your lifestyle, which includes good nutrition and enough exercise, and you should definitely keep it that way, even if it sometimes requires a lot of discipline in your stressful daily life. Also try to work a little on your bad habits. 2024 will give you the necessary strength to do so.

August / September

CW 35	♍	**Virgo** *24.08. – 22.09.*
Mon 26	☽	half moon waning, St. Louis
Tue 27 -	♂ ☾	✝ Great Martyr Fanourios
Wed 28	☿ ☾	💎 St. Augustine Feast Day (Isleta Pueblo)
Thu 29	♃ ☾	✝ Beheading of the Holy and Glorious Prophet, Forerunner and Baptist John
Fri 30	♀ ☾	St. Felix
Sat 31 -	♄ ☾	✝ The Placing of the Honorable Sash of the Most Holy Virgin Theotokos Mother Mary
Sun 1	☉ ☾	St. Aegidius

Monthly trend September	love	friends, family	profession, money
Aries	☼☼☼☼	☼☼☼	☼☼☼
Taurus	☼☼☼☼☼☼	☼	☼☼☼☼☼☼
Gemini	☼☼	☼☼☼☼☼☼	☼☼☼☼☼
Cancer	☼☼☼☼	☼	☼☼☼☼☼☼
Leo	☼	☼☼☼☼☼☼	☼☼
Virgo	☼☼☼☼	☼☼	☼☼☼☼☼☼
Libra	☼☼☼☼☼☼	☼☼☼☼☼☼	☼☼
Scorpio	☼☼☼☼☼☼	☼	☼☼☼☼☼☼
Sagittarius	☼☼	☼☼	☼☼☼☼
Capricorn	☼☼☼☼☼☼	☼	☼☼☼
Aquarius	☼☼	☼☼☼☼☼☼	☼
Pisces	☼☼	☼☼☼☼☼☼	☼☼☼☼☼☼

Lucid dreaming

Lucid dreams are different from ordinary dreams and are probably more of the extraordinary experiences of perception that a person can have. What is meant by lucid dreaming? When we dream lucidly, we are suddenly aware that we are dreaming. If we have mastered lucid dreaming, then we can decide at that time to wake up or to continue dreaming. In lucid dreaming, we can influence the dream happening consciously. We know that we ourselves have created the dream world we are experiencing. And we can change the laws that regulate the dream world to our liking. We can fly and use superpowers. We can face situations that burden us in waking life through possibilities that we have only in dreams, and in this way, for example, reduce fears. Or we can duel with an opposing person who makes life difficult for us. Maybe we will meet him with more self-confidence in the future. We can even use dreams effectively: In a lucid dream, we can specifically train skills (giving a lecture for example) that we need in our real life. Lucid dreaming helps with self-optimization and has a positive effect on personality. It is said that it helps to improve performance, concentration and creativity. Anything is possible in lucid dreaming.

> Like normal dreaming, lucid dreaming also takes place in the last sleep phase, the so-called REM sleep phase (REM stands for "Rapid Eye Movement").
> It is the last of a total of five phases of a sleep cycle: 1. non-REM sleep / 2. falling asleep phase / 3. light sleep / 4. deep sleep / 5. dream sleep (REM sleep)
>
> While in the non-REM sleep phase the brain activity and brain waves are shut down, what is special about the REM sleep phase is that they are more active again and almost as high as when awake.

So one way of lucid dreaming is to recognize during normal dreaming that we are lucid dreaming and then consciously intervene in the further dream happening. The other, more difficult way, is to go from a conscious dream imagination, which we bring to our mind's eye, directly from the full waking state without interruption of consciousness into the lucid dream. This has the advantage that we can imagine exactly THAT situation which torments us, for example, and then work on it in lucid dreaming.

There are actually only a few people who can lucid dream simply by nature. So how can we learn lucid dreaming? Eating or smoking special herbs, burning incense, smells and sounds can help to open the gateway to lucid dreaming more easily and to enter a parallel matrix, a parallel world or universe where anything is possible.

$$\Omega \; \Omega \; \Omega$$

Anyone who wants to learn lucid dreaming should definitely keep a **dream diary**, adopt a **sleep mantra** and perform **reality checks** at regular intervals. A **healthy diet and good, adequate sleep** are also helpful. These are the points that summarize the best known and easiest to learn method for lucid dreaming. It is known as the **MILD method** and was developed by the American psychologist Stephen LaBerge. **MILD stands for "Mnemonic Induction of Lucid Dreams".**

1. Keep dream diary
Immediately after waking up, we write down the dreams we can remember in a dream journal. When we then lie in bed in the evening, we read our written-down dream again and so virtually relive it a second time. This is to stimulate our brain to process the dream more intensively: a first important step in preparing for the control of dreams.

2. Sleep mantra before going to sleep
A second helpful step on the way to lucid dreaming is to practice our own sleep mantra. We say this to ourselves directly before falling asleep, for example, "I remember my dreams as soon as I wake up."

3. Regular implementation of reality checks
It is also recommended to perform reality checks on a regular basis. The basic requirement for lucid dreaming is that during the dream we are aware that we are dreaming. Therefore, we should practice being aware of reality while awake. We can do this easily by holding our nose, which makes breathing more difficult, which in turn would not be a problem in the dream.

4. healthy diet and good, adequate sleep

A balanced diet is very important for a good night's sleep. It is also good not to eat anything directly before going to bed, and even the evening meal should not be very lavish. The deep sleep phase is a prerequisite for dreaming in the subsequent dream sleep phase. Among other things, a well-balanced hormone balance is important for this, especially the substance Melatonin, which is responsible for our day-night rhythm. When it gets dark, our body produces Melatonin, which makes us tired and ensures restful sleep. If we cannot produce enough Melantonin ourselves (often the case with older people), appropriate dietary supplements can help. Natural substances, such as extracts from lemon balm or passion flower, can also promote sleep.

Who can be sure which reality is the right one? Do you really know exactly whether you are awake right now and not dreaming? Surely most would say quite spontaneously: "Yes of course I am awake now and in reality and not in a dream. What a question!" But what if you were leading a parallel life in your dreams, which you also believe to be real there? Don't you sometimes feel that you remember certain places, smells, feelings, but you don't find these memories in your real life?

*The world of dreams is so fascinating. It fascinates me so much that I have been working for many years on a big **Book of dreams** with very detailed dream interpretation, which is now close to completion.*

Morpheus

September

CW 36	♍	**_Virgo_** *24.08. – 22.09.* 🌿 **_Willow - tree of vitality:_** *03. - 12.09.*
Mon 2	☾)	💎 San Estevan Feast Day
Tue 3	♂ ☉	new moon
Wed 4 -	☿)	St. Rosalia
Thu 5	♃)	✝ Holy Prophet Zacharias, Father of the Venerable Forerunner
Fri 6 +	♀)	St. Magnus
Sat 7	♄)	St. Regine
Sun 8	☉)	✝ The nativity of our Holy Lady, the Theotokos and ever Virgin Mary – 💎 is also celebrated by the Laguna Pueblo, World Literacy Day

Properties and effects of the moon phases in relation to health and medicines

Waxing Moon:
Uplifting, absorbing, storing energy. This is the time to give something to the body, to strengthen it.

Waning Moon:
Exhaling, sweating out, draining energy. At this time, healing takes place faster than usual. Examinations and schoolwork proceed more favorably during this time. Even with increased appetite, you do not increase weight or only a little during this time. It is a good time for operations.

New moon to full moon:
All stimulants work better and faster. Tranquilizers, on the other hand, work more slowly, sometimes not at all.

Full moon:
Body temperature is higher than normal. People with a tendency to nervousness and hysteria are especially sensitive to this around the time of the full moon. Medicinal herbs collected at full moon are particularly effective.

New Moon:
Diets on new moon promise the greatest success, because then the readiness of the body to detoxify is particularly high. Giving up vices (such as smoking) on new moon days is said to have the greatest chance of sustainability.

Moon change:
Operations should not be performed in times of the moon change.

Moon in conjunction with Saturn:
Stimulants (substances that have an excitatory effect on cells, organs or the whole organism) lose their effect or have only a very weak effect. A disease that takes its beginning in this period will be of long duration.

Moon in conjunction with Mars:
All remedies respond well.

$$\Omega \diamondsuit \Omega$$

The shortest words
- namely yes and no -
require the most thought.

Pythagoras

September

CW 37	♍	**Virgo** 24.08. – 22.09.
		🌿 *Linden tree - Tree of harmony:* 13. - 22.09.
Mon 9	☾	St. Gorgon
Tue 10 +	♂	† *Martyrs Menodora, Metrodora and Nymphodora*, World Suicide Prevention Day
Wed 11 -	☿	half moon waxing, † *Theodora of Alexandria*, St. Protus
Thu 12	♃	Mary's Name Day
Fri 13 +	♀	Feast of the goddess Aphrodite
Sat 14	♄	† *The elevation of the venerable and life-giving cross*
Sun 15	☉	† *Great Martyr Nikitas*, **I** *Mawlid an-Nabi (+ 16.09.)*

~ 109 ~

Goddess Aphrodite

13. September honors Aphrodite, the Greek goddess of beauty and love. She is responsible for the heavenly as well as sensual love.

She is one of the twelve Olympian deities and has the nickname "The Foamborn", which goes back to her birth from the waves of the sea, into which the penis and sperm of the emasculated Uranus had fallen.

Aphrodite

Aphrodite and what suits her

Day: Friday / **Angels: Anael**, Rachiel, Sachiel / **Olympian spirit:** Hagith / **Organs:** kidneys, skin, organs of equilibrium / **Mental aspects:** love, harmonious togetherness, friendship, sexuality / **Chakra:** heart / **Zodiac signs:** Taurus and Libra / **Colors:** pink, copper / **Metal:** copper / **Animals:** bull, rooster, dog seal, sparrow, rock dove, panther, goat / **Woods, trees:** myrtle bush, birch / **Plants, herbs:** myrtle, celandine, true coriander, forget-me-not, Easter lucerne, verbena, pomegranate / **Incense, oils:** musk, myrtle, amber, aloe wood, coral dust / **Healing stones:** emerald, amethyst, chrysolite, beryllium

The hours of Aphrodite are suitable for all rituals related to love, eroticism, partnership, beauty and harmony.

Selene and what suits her

Day: Monday / **Angels: Gabriel**, Vileth, Missalno / **Olympian spirit:** Phul /
Organs: stomach, spleen, uterus, autonomic nervous system, left eye / **Mental aspects:** unconscious, intuition, perceptions / **Chakra:** forehead / **Zodiac sign:** Cancer / **Colors:** purple, white, silver / **Metal:** silver / **Animals:** dog, cat, goose, crayfish, pheasant, cow / **Woods, trees:** willow, cherry, sandalwood tree, linden / **Plants, herbs:** camphora, white water lily, white poppy seeds, red cloves / **Incense, oils:** camphora, water lily, poppy seeds, clove, sandalwood, frog eggs, bull's eyes / **Healing stones:** pearl, pink chalcopyrite, moonstone, rock crystal

The lessons of Selene are suitable for topics related to women, domestic issues, spiritual development and purification, letting go of negative aspects and new beginnings / changes, as well as incantations and rituals involving hatred and enmity.

September

CW 38	♍	*Virgo* 24.08. – 22.09.
Mo 16	☾ ●	† *Great Martyr Euphemia*, St. Cyrianus
Tue 17	♂ ●	Lunar eclipse (partial, 17. > 18.09.)
Wed 18 +	☿ ○	full moon: Corn Moon
Thu 19	♃ ●	💎 St. Joseph's Feast Day (Laguna Pueblo)
Fri 20	♀ ●	St. Eustachius
Sat 21	♄ ●	International Peace Day, St. Matthäus
Sun 22	☉ ●	St. Mauritius † Βοηδρομιών †

~ 111 ~

September Full Moon

Corn Moon

The Native American Indigenous call the Full Moon in September "Corn Moon" because corn is harvested during this month. They also refer to it as the "Harvest Moon."

Helios and what suits him

Day: Sunday / **Angels:** Michael, Dardael, Urdaphil / **Olympian spirit:** Och / **Organs:** brain, heart, circulation, right eye / **Mental aspects:** healing, spiritual development, self-realization / **Chakras:** Crown and Heart / **Zodiac Sign:** Leo / **Colors:** orange, yellow / **Metal:** gold / **Animals:** lion, eagle, swan, white rooster, nightingale, lark / **Woods, trees:** laurel, ash, amber tree, orange tree / **Plants, herbs:** clove, aloe, St. John's wort, cinnamon, sunflower (seeds) / **Incense, oils:** vlove, myrrh, gum resin, amber, musk, aloe wood / **Healing stones:** diamond, zircon, lapis lazuli

The hours of Helios are suitable for light-bringing magical works, for love, pleasure, social events and everything extraordinary.

Zeus and what fits him

Day: Thursday / **Angels:** Sachiel, Kassiel, Asaiel / **Olympian spirit:** Bethor / **Organs:** liver, connective tissue, arteries, heart (with sun) / **Mental aspects:** foresight, spiritual goals, living flow of all energies / **Chakras:** forehead and solar plexus / **Zodiac signs:** Sagittarius and Pisces / **Color:** blue / **Metals:** tin, zinc / **Animals:** ox, elephant, peacock, pheasant, dolphin, barn swallow, deer / **Woods, trees:** Greco-Rumelian pine, maple, ash, elm, poplar, sycamore / **Plants, herbs:** aloe, strawflower, jasmine, viola (horned violet), sesame / **Incense, oils:** common ash seed, aloe wood, storax resin (styrax), gum resin, cornflower / **Healing stones:** sapphire, lapis lazuli, carnelian, flint

The hours of Zeus are suitable for magical work and rituals that serve growth, healing and inner strength. It is the time for optimistic planning, the start of important things, as well as religion and philosophy.

September

CW 39	♎	**Libra** 23.09. – 22.10.
		🌿 *Olive tree – Tree of wisdom:* 23.09 / 🌿 *Hazel – Tree of truth:* 24.09 - 03.10.
Mon 23	☾ ◐	Mabon, equinox, beginning of autumn, Libra > 22.10. ☦ *Conception of St. John, the Baptist*
Tue 24	♂ ◐	**half moon waning**, ☦ *commemoration of the miracle of the Theotokos Myrtidiotissis in Kythyra*
Wed 25	☿ ☾	💎 *St. Elisabeth Feast Day*, Native American Day
Thu 26	♃ ☾	☦ *The falling asleep of St. John, the Evangelist and Theologian* St. Damian, St. Cosmas
Fri 27 -	♀ ☾	
Sat 28	♄ ☾	
Sun 29	☉ ☾	Archangel Michel (Michael's Day), 💎 *San Geronimo Festival Evening (Taos Pueblo)*

Mabon 23. *September*

Mabon celebrates the end of the harvest season and the equinox at the same time. **Day and night are of equal length and the sun is 0 degrees in the zodiac sign Libra.** Therefore, Mabon is also a celebration of (inner) harmony and balance. The central event of the pagan autumn festival is a rich meal to give thanks for the good harvest. As a sign of gratitude, three fruits are thrown over one's shoulder in honor of the corn mother. During the grain harvest, the last sheaf is left tied together or not cut at all.

On Mabon, God Sun retires and prepares for his death (and rebirth). With him, nature prepares for winter, the dead time. Thus, this festival also represents the farewell to summer and serves as an inward preparation for winter. On this day, people pause and reflect on what has happened in the past year in order to be ready for the coming year. A Mabon meal includes venison, red wines, melons, cakes and anything that can be made from apples. The altar is decorated with acorns, pinecones and autumn leaves. Smoking is done with myrrh, sage and pine. Colors: dark red, brown.

The 12 houses in astrology and the horoscope

The astrological system of houses is important basis of the horoscope. Each house has its own meaning and stands for a certain area of life.

House	represents	is under the sign
1.	personality and attitude to life	Aries
2.	acquisition and possession	Taurus
3.	communication and learning	Gemini
4.	origin and family	Cancer
5.	creativity and pleasure	Leo
6.	everyday life and professional life	Virgo
7.	relationship and partnership	Libra
8.	boundary experiences and devotion, transformation, change	Scorpio
9.	expansion of the horizon, spiritual growth	Sagittarius
10.	publicity, achievement, profession, reputation, social position, influence, power, honor	Capricorn
11.	friendship and visions, realization of one's own wishes	Aquarius
12.	spirituality, transcendental, dreams, inspiration, cosmic consciousness	Pisces

In In interaction with the planets, statements can be made about the personality.

For example, Aphrodite in the 1st house means: You are very charming and your personality has charisma, which fascinates many. You are very sensitive and have the ability to say always exactly the right thing to "captivate" people around you.

Libra 23.09. – 22.10.

The zodiac sign of Libra embodies romance, sympathy, friendliness and relaxation. Libra people can be indecisive, overly calm and sometimes mischievous.

Good time for magical work related to
justice, emotional or spiritual balance, karmic connections / entanglements, as well as partnership and creativity / artistic.

Planet: Aphrodite (Venus) / **Angel:** Anael / **Olympian spirit:** Hagith / **Element:** Air / **Lucky Stones:** Coral, Diamond, Sapphire, Jade / **Colors: pink**, sky blue, turquoise / **Lucky Day:** Friday / **Lucky Numbers:** 5, 25, 35 / **Flowers:** lily, rose, daffodil, violet / **Metal:** copper / **Animals:** dove, nightingale, swan, flamingo / **Affected body parts:** Kidneys, bladder, sense of balance, skin

Libra in 2024

In 2024, there will be events that aim to permanently change your mentality and question your previous life planning. In the period from the beginning of March to the end of May it becomes apparent – possibly due to an important message – that things will start to look up for you from now on, provided that you take advantage of the opportunities that present themselves to you. To do this, however, you will have to detach yourself from the past. July and October will bring major positive changes. The doors to success will be wide open for you and opportunities for advancement and expansion will arise at any time. You have prioritized practical problems and put emotional "building sites" on ice for the moment, because 2024 will give you the will to create a successful and independent life for yourself, so that you don't have to depend on anyone. Try to become more independent and build lasting and meaningful relationships with the people around you. This way you will always find guidance and help when you face challenges. Stay true to your desires, don't compromise and live on your own terms as long as you don't harm anyone around you. Put honesty first, celebrate your successes every step of the way, and lay a solid foundation for your future. Use your creative abilities to successfully achieve your goals especially at the professional level.

The year 2024 awakens your longing for freedom and adventure and good times. It also promises you to be the year of relationships and social activities. However, it is important to preserve your individuality and not let yourself be manipulated. Also, when looking for a partner, choose wisely and do not rush into anything. From March, you should put all your energy into realizing your plans and goals, and this will be easier with the support of your friends. In April the pressure you will feel will decrease and your partnership will also improve. Especially in summer until early autumn you will meet interesting people and make alliances.

Libra: love, family and friends

In 2024 you should spend more time with your partner and do everything to get closer (again). In the first three months of the year, you will have an easy time attracting the attention of others because of your strong powers of attraction. With your charm you enchant your partner. Or are you still looking for your suitable partner? Then the months of January to March are an ideal time for it.

Singles among those born under the Libra zodiac sign are lucky in the emotional sphere all year round and especially in the months of July and October. You will meet interesting people who will attract your attention in unexpected places. Before rushing into a relationship, however, make sure you are truly ready to accept and welcome the love in your heart. A strong need for creativity and new interests will lead you to seek out people who can offer you not only thrills, but also guarantees of honest and stable togetherness. In October you will be reminded that friends are a very important chapter in your life. They will help you find a solution to your love problems. This will give you self-esteem and self-confidence, which in turn will help you in your search for a partner.

The accumulated family problems will make you want adventure, freedom and independence. Some family members will rebel and demand more commitment from you for the family. You must find a way to bring peace back to your family, but without putting your own concerns completely on the back burner.

You love to retreat and enjoy spending time alone. But don't forget that you also need other people to get new impulses. Choose them carefully. Then you will experience how they become trusted companions and stand rock solid by your side, especially in times when you are emotionally unbalanced.

Libra: profession and finances

In 2024, you will have to fight for justice at work. Your professional life requires a lot of prudence and flexibility this year. Make sure that you fulfill your obligations consistently and correctly so that you cannot be attacked. Developing your career will take some time and may almost make you despair and give up. You should not force anything, but be patient until things fall into place so that you are satisfied with them.

2024 opens a new path to improving your finances, but it will not be quick or sudden, but slow and gradual. Your financial situation continues to experience ups and downs and it is possible that a major unforeseen expense will unsettle you.

Be careful especially in the times of lunar eclipses (in March, September and October), because there is a threat of financial losses. From June onwards, your financial circumstances will improve and you will also be able to build up reserves more easily. In 2024, you may take several business trips where you will meet new investors who will be excited about your plans. Find new income opportunities. Zeus will help you do this, especially in the second half of the year.

Libra: health

Your health will be average to good in 2024. Protect yourself especially from viruses and diseases during the time when Hermes is retrograde (in April, in August and from late November to mid-December). It will be very important to watch your diet.

September / October

CW 40	♎	**Libra** 23.09. – 22.10.
		🌳 **Mountain ash - Tree of vitality:** 04. - 13.10.
Mon 30 +	☾ ☾	💎 San Geronimo Feast Day (Taos Pueblo), St. Hieronymus
Tue 1	♂ ☾	St. Remigius † Ἐλευσίνια Μυστήρια †
Wed 2	☿ ☉	**new moon, solar eclipse** (annular), ✝ St. Cyprian and St. Justine, **J** Rosh ha-Shanah (until 04.10.), International Day of Non-Violence
Thu 3 -	♃ ☽	
Fri 4	♀ ☽	Feast of St. Francis of Assisi 💎 *is also celebrated by the Nambe Pueblo*
Sat 5	♄ ☽	**J** Zom Gedaliah
Sun 6	☉ ☽	✝ *The Holy and Glorious Apostle Thomas*

~ 117 ~

Monthly trend October	love	friends, family	profession, money
Aries	☼☼☼☼☼	☼☼☼☼☼	☼
Taurus	☼	☼☼☼☼☼	☼☼☼☼☼
Gemini	☼☼☼☼☼	☼☼☼☼	☼
Cancer	☼	☼☼☼☼☼	☼☼☼
Leo	☼☼☼☼☼	☼☼	☼☼
Virgo	☼☼☼☼☼	☼☼☼☼☼	☼☼
Libra	☼☼	☼☼☼☼☼	☼☼☼☼
Scorpio	☼☼☼☼☼	☼	☼☼☼☼☼
Sagittarius	☼☼☼☼☼	☼☼☼☼☼	☼☼
Capricorn	☼☼	☼☼☼☼	☼☼☼☼☼
Aquarius	☼☼☼☼☼	☼	☼☼☼☼☼
Pisces	☼☼☼☼☼	☼☼☼☼☼	☼

Witch broom ritual to get rid of unwanted guests

To get rid of unwanted guests and those who don't notice when it's time to leave, there is a simple but very effective magic spell. All you need is your witches' broom. If you want your guests finally to leave your house, then do the following. Leave the room where your guests are staying under a pretext and close the door. Place your witches' broom on the floor with the handle pointing towards the door. Alternatively, you can hold it in your hands. However, the handle must still be pointing towards the door.

Then stand behind your broom and quietly sing the following:

Rentum Scorbium Araculum !
Get out of my house through that door.
I want to rest now.
You have no more time and must go now.
Go right now, your time is up !
Rentum Scorbium Araculum !

Take a few relaxed breaths in and out intensely imagine your guests leaving. Then put your broom back in its place. Now go back inside to your guests and secretly look forward to them saying goodbye in 15 minutes at the latest.

October

CW 41	♎	*Libra* 23.09. – 22.10.
Mon 7	☾	
Tue 8	♂	St. Pelagia
Wed 9 -	☿	St. Dionysius
Thu 10	♃	**half moon waxing**, World Mental Health Day
Fri 11	♀	Feast of the goddess Demeter, *Yom Kippur (+ 12.10.)*
Sat 12	♄	
Sun 13 +	☉	

Goddess Demeter

The Greek goddess is responsible for the fertility of the earth, the grain, the seed and the seasons. Demeter is the Earth goddess. She is equated with Ceres from the Roman period.

Prayer to Demeter
(Aradia, Artemis, Astarte)

Sailing your course around the heaven,
flowing through all, shining for all,
light of the world.
You virgin, mother, old lady,
green proliferator, weaver,
Isis, Astarte, Ishtar, Aradia,
Diana, Cybele, Kore,
Cerridwen, Levanah, Luna,
Mari, Anna, Rhiannon,
Selene, Demeter.

See with our eyes, hear with our ears,
touch with our hands,
breathe through our noses,
kiss with our lips.
Open our hearts, fill us, touch us,
transform us, heal us!

Ω ◇ Ω

*Everything that humans are doing to the animals,
returns to the humans again.*

Pythagoras

October

CW 42	♎	**_Libra_** 23.09. – 22.10.
		🍁 *Maple - Tree of freedom:* 14. - 23.10.
Mon 14	☾	St. Burkhard
	●	
Tue 15	♂	St. Theresa
	●	
Wed 16 +	☿	**J** *Sukkot (through Oct. 23)*, World Food Day, St. Longinus, St. Hedwig, St. Gallus
	●	
Thu 17	♃	**full moon: Hunter's Moon, Lunar eclipse** (almost total),
	○	💎 *St. Margaret Mary's Feast Day,* International Day for the Eradication of Poverty
Fri 18	♀	St. Lukas
	●	
Sat 19	♄	
	●	
Sun 20	☉	St. Wendelin
	●	

October full moon

Hunter's Moon

In autumn the Native American Indigenous traditionally prepared
for winter and stocked up on meat. For this reason,
they also call the full moon in October "Hunter's Moon".
Sometimes they also call it "Harvest Moon",
like the full moon in September.

Greek deities

Ancient Greece and the Roman Empire had a strong influence on each other, so that the world of the gods of the two empires is also closely interwoven. Most of the Greek deities therefore have Roman counterparts.

Cronos (Saturn): Son of Gaia (earth) and Uranos (heaven), leader of the Titans, father of Zeus, personification of time.
Zeus (Jupiter): God of the sky, king of the Olympian gods.
Hera (Juno): Goddess of women, queen of the Olympian gods.
Apollo: God of light (the sun), arts, music, divination and healing.
Artemis (Diana): Goddess of the hunt, the moon and the life cycle (sister of Apollo).
Hermes (Mercury): God of communication (messenger of the gods), guides souls to the afterlife.
Athena (Minerva): Goddess of wisdom, war (without aggression).
Ares (Mars): God of war, violence and passion (son of Zeus and Hera).
Aphrodite (Venus): Goddess of beauty, love and sexuality.
Dionysus (Bacchus): God of wine, pleasure, powerful life and primal instincts.
Demeter (Ceres): Goddess of the fertility of the earth.
Poseidon (Neptune): God of the sea and water in general.
Persephone: Goddess of fertility (like her mother Demeter) and the underworld.
Hades (Pluto): God of the underworld, lord of the dead and God of wealth.
Hecate: Goddess of the moon and magic and also of the underworld.
Panas: God of wild landscapes, animals and shepherds.
Hestia: Goddess of the house and hearth, responsible for tranquility and material abundance.
Asclepius: God of medicine and healing (son of Apollo).
Hephaestus: God of fire and metalworking (son of Zeus and Hera).

Akropolis

October

CW 43	♏	**Scorpio** 23.10. – 22.11. (previously Libra)
		🌿 *Walnut - Tree of new beginnings:* 24.10. - 11.11.
Mon 21 +	☾	
Tue 22	♂	J *Hoschana Rabba (+ 23.10.)* † Πυανέψια †
Wed 23	☿	J *Shmini Azeret (until 25.10.)*, St Severin Scorpio > 22.11.
Thu 24	♃	half moon waning, J *Simchat Torah (+ 25.10.)* † Θησεία † St. Raphael
Fri 25 +	♀	St. Crispinus † Θεσμοφόρεια †
Sat 26	♄	✝ *The Holy and Great Martyr Demetrios,* *the Myrrh Streamer*
Sun 27 -	☉	Beginning of winter time

Scorpio 23.10. - 22.11.

People born under the sign of Scorpio live intensely, have strong feelings and act purposefully. Jealousy, hatred and resentful behavior are also typical for the Scorpio.

Good time for magical work dealing with all aspects of power, sexuality, psychic growth, secrets and fundamental transformations

Planets: Ares (Mars) and Pluto / **Angel:** Samael / **Olympian spirit:** Phaleg / **Element:** water / **Lucky stones:** coral, ruby, topaz / **Colors:** black, ocher yellow, olive green, fuchsia, violet / **Lucky day:** Tuesday / **Lucky numbers:** 7, 47, 87 / **Flowers:** orchid, gardenia, dahlia / **Metals:** platinum, iron / **Animals:** mole, snake, dormouse / **Body parts influenced:** nose, genitals, large intestine, rectum, blood, ureter, back

Scorpio in 2024

The year 2024 serves as a preparatory year for you for major changes that will take place in your near future. Pluto's cautionary entry into Aquarius speaks of the establishment of a new way of life that you will embrace beginning in 2025. You will use past experiences to slowly and steadily prepare for this new way of life, which may include a new career. 2024 will be full of warning omens and protective events for you, which will help you to enter the new phase of your life on a good and safe path and strengthened in soul and spirit. You will have the necessary strength and energy to move forward with your plans. Believe in yourself and discover how much better you can make your life. Work to achieve stability in all areas of your life.

2024 will be a very successful year for those born under the zodiac sign Scorpio, in terms of career and lifestyle. Luck will accompany you throughout the year, but this does not mean that all months will go smoothly. For example, at the beginning of the year, the family atmosphere may be somewhat marred by the negative attitude of some family members. You will also be worried about your professional prospects in the first months of the year, but if you keep your outlook beyond your own nose and are open to new and perhaps unconventional things, you will overcome all difficulties and move forward optimistically. The best months to work on realizing your plans and goals are April, May and August. From March onwards, you will get the right support and help from friends that you need to move forward with new projects. Zeus will be your great sponsor in the financial field, especially in the second half of the year, because a great flow of money awaits you there. You will have a good year in 2024, but you should be careful with your decisions and take things slowly in your life. Be patient and you will soon be able to reap the fruits of your labor.

Scorpio: love, family and friends

If you are in a partnership that works and fulfills you, do everything you can in 2024 to intensify and strengthen it. Try to always focus on each other and find out together how you can make your love life even more interesting. However, if you perceive disturbing feelings in your relationship, do not ignore them. The year 2024 is the year of changes and will help you take the step out of a worn out relationship. For singles who want a relationship, 2024 brings a romantic beginning with a new partner.

Within the family, especially at the beginning of the year, there will be conflicts and perhaps even a break with family members. The only thing that helps here at the moment is distance. Let go, better times will come again. However, it is important that you do not withdraw from your responsibilities and obligations to your family. Still be there for them when they need you.

In 2024, to improve your life on a social level, it is essential that you learn to accept and respect other people's opinions. You cannot always be right. Listen to others and don't just talk about yourself. In this way, you will quickly realize who could be your ideal companion in this time of change and support you in your future plans. You will have the chance of a new acquaintance with a person who has the same values and ideals as you. However, caution is advised in May, because you tend to be very selfish and demanding, which may destroy newly established friendships.

Scorpio: profession and finances

There is a strong wind of optimism blowing in your professional interests in 2024. You will make great professional progress as long as you continue to work hard and do not waste time on useless matters. Set strict priorities and give energy and attention only to the tasks and projects that will move you forward. 2024 marks the beginning of a new professional era that will gradually reveal itself in the coming years. If you are thinking about starting a business, 2024 is the best time to do it. Dare to take the step up the professional ladder or even into self-employment: 2024 is a very favorable year to start your own business. But inform yourself well about the risks beforehand. On a professional level, there will also be no shortage of support from people well-disposed towards you. From May, people will enter your life with whom you cooperate very well. You will help each other to move forward. Each helps the other with his own competences.

Your financial situation will relax at the beginning of March, because you will manage to permanently reduce your current personal and family expenses. Most of the year will be profitable and you will be able to afford many things you have long wanted. However, even in a time of financial abundance, it is important to save and create reserves.
Also look into possibilities of financial investments, for example, buying shares.

Scorpio: health

To keep yourself healthy, you need to be a little more disciplined about eating and staying fit. Regular exercise, movement in the fresh air and a balanced diet will strengthen your immune system and help you meet the challenges of 2024. Even if you find it hard to stick to a fitness program at first, you'll soon realize how good it is for you and what was initially a chore will turn into a nice routine you can't imagine doing without.

October / November

CW 44	♏	**Scorpio** 23.10. – 22.11.
Mon 28	☽	✝ *Protection and intercession of the Theotokos Holy Mary, Apostles Simon and Judas*
Tue 29	♂ ☾	
Wed 30	☿ ☾	
Thu 31 +	♃ ☾	Halloween
Fri 1 +	♀ ☉	**Samhain, All Saints Day**, mid-autumn, **H** *Diwali (Deepavali)*, new moon
Sat 2	♄ ☽	All Souls' Day
Sun 3	☉ ☽	✝ Οσχοφόρια ✝

Monthly trend November	love	friends, family	profession, money
Aries	☼	☼☼☼☼☼	☼☼☼
Taurus	☼☼☼☼☼	☼☼☼	☼
Gemini	☼☼☼☼☼	☼☼☼☼☼	☼
Cancer	☼	☼☼	☼☼☼☼☼
Leo	☼☼☼	☼☼☼☼	☼☼
Virgo	☼☼☼	☼☼	☼
Libra	☼☼☼☼☼	☼☼☼	☼☼
Scorpio	☼	☼☼	☼☼
Sagittarius	☼	☼☼☼☼☼	☼
Capricorn	☼☼☼☼☼	☼☼☼☼	☼☼
Aquarius	☼☼	☼☼	☼☼
Pisces	☼☼☼	☼☼	☼☼☼☼☼

Samhain 1. *November*

On the harvest festival of Samhain, God Sun leaves his body and sinks into darkness for a while. With Samhain, the Celtic year came to an end. Since the new year did not begin until the next morning, the night was regarded as an interim period in which the boundaries between the "Otherworld" and ours were transparent: Spirits walked around and it was possible to see into the future by oracles. This is why Samhain is also known as the Day of the dead.

It was celebrated with great fires and processions. Sacrifices were made to the gods (including Samhain, the god of the dead): crops, animals, even people (criminals, prisoners or first-born children). There are many traditions on Samhain, for example lighting a white candle for each dead person and letting it burn until it goes out by itself. A warm red wine spiced with cinnamon, cloves, ginger and nutmeg is a traditional drink on Samhain. In the evening, a meal for the souls that are supposed to be on their way that night can be placed in front of the house, lit by a candle or lamp, so that the souls can find their way. A warm red wine spiced with cinnamon, cloves, ginger and nutmeg is a traditional drink for Samhain. The altar is decorated with pumpkins, nuts, autumnal flowers and photos of deceased. In addition, there is often a dark mirror on it for contacting the deceased. Incense: nutmeg, sage or mint.

November

CW 45	♏	**Scorpio** *23.10. – 22.11.*
Mon 4	☾ ☽	
Tue 5	♂ ☽	
Wed 6 -	☿ ☽	
Thu 7	♃ ☽	Birthday of Baha'u'llah – Baha'i
Fri 8	♀ ☽	✝ Synaxis of the Holy Archangels Michael, Gabriel and other heavenly powers
Sat 9	♄ ◐	half moon waxing
Sun 10	☉ ◑	✝ St. Arsenius, the Cappadocian, World Day of Science for Peace and Development

The magic of trees

Since the beginning of time, people have been fascinated by trees and their elemental power. Whether as a whole forest or just as a single tree. Many plantings and ancient traditions have their roots in the deep knowledge of the far-reaching effects and significance of trees. Anyone who engages with ancient tree knowledge will quickly feel that trees are so much more than mere useful plants. They were and are "mediators" between heaven and earth as well as protectors and guardians of sacred places. By the way, this applies not only to the living tree, but also to the special woods they provide us with:

Alder helps us gain self-confidence, clarity and perseverance.

Apple tree gives wisdom and promises long life (tree of immortality).

Ash brings protection, prosperity and health.

Birch helps new beginnings, gives vitality, connects the worlds of life and death.

Cherry represents love, fertility, but also separation, death and rebirth.

Elder helps with transformation and protects the home.

Fir gives grounding, gives protection and provides honesty.

Hawthorn provides purification, gives strength and keeps away negativity.

Linde provides sociability, social integration and justice.

Maple gives cheerfulness, lightness, tolerance and serenity.

Mistletoe helps visions and reveals past lives.

Oak gives healing, strength and wisdom.

Pine promises prosperity and growth.

Poplar awakens understanding of the grand plan, assists in spiritual development.

Willow invites the goddess to fulfill wishes, inspires and gives balance.

November

CW 46	♏	**Scorpio** *23.10. – 22.11.*
		Chestnut - Tree of openness: 12. - 21.11.
Mon 11	☾ ●	St. Martin ⸸ Ἀπατούρια ⸸
Tue 12	♂ ●	💎 San Diego Feast Day (Tesuque & Jemez Pueblos)
Wed 13 +	☿ ●	
Thu 14	♃ ●	
Fri 15	♀ ○	full moon: Beaver Moon ⸸ Χαλκεῖα ⸸
Sat 16	♄ ●	International Day for Tolerance ⸸ Μαιμακτηριών ⸸
Sun 17	☉ ●	

November Full Moon

Beaver Moon

In preparation for the harsh winter season the Native American Indigenous
set traps in November to catch beavers and other fur-bearing animals
in order to have enough warming pelts.
This is the basis for the name "Beaver Moon".

Hermes and what suits him

Day: Wednesday / **Angels: Raphael**, Miel, Seraphiel / **Olympian spirit**: Ophiel / **Organs:** nerves, spinal cord, hormones, metabolism / **Mental aspects:** mediator between body, mind and soul / **Chakra:** Throat / **Zodiac Sign:** Gemini and Virgo / **Colors:** yellow, copper / **Metals:** copper, mercury / **Animals:** monkey, parrot, fox, dog, weasel, jay / **Woods, trees:** walnut, elm, acacia / **Plants, herbs:** anise, bloodroot, honeysuckle, clove, mastic pistachio, stonecrop / **Incense, oils:** mastic resin (best from the Greek island of Chios), gum resin, clove, bloodroot, agate powder / **Healing stones**: agate, carnelian, opal, onyx

The hours of Hermes are suitable for communication, togetherness, mental alertness, presentation and persuasion, contracting, professional success and travel.
They are also suitable for summoning medium spirits.

Yesterday is gone.
Tomorrow is not here.
So live today!
Pythagoras

November

CW 47	♐	**Sagittarius** 23.11. - 21.12. (previously Scorpio)
		🌿 *Ash tree - Tree of energy: 22.11. - 01.12.*
Mon 18	☾	World Day of Philosophy
Tue 19	♂	St. Elisabeth
Wed 20	☿	Day of Prayer and Repentance, World Children's Day
Thu 21	♃	✝ The entrance of the Theotokos into the temple, ✝ Saint Elder Iakovos Tsalikis
Fri 22	♀	St. Cecilia
Sat 23 +	♄	**half moon waning**, St. Clement Sagittarius > 21.12.
Sun 24	☉	

~ 132 ~

The very special meaning of the trees for the Celts

In Celtic mythology, trees were given a special meaning. In the culture, which is more than 2000 years old, trees were seen as sacred and had healing properties. Their entire lives were influenced by the magic of trees. This is probably most clearly seen in the tree calendar, in which each month is assigned to a tree and a specific time. The full moons of the Celtic months also have the names of the corresponding trees:

Month of the	Time	Name of the month
Birch	24.12. - 20.01.	Beth / Birch Moon
Rowan	21.01. - 17.02.	Luis / Rowan Moon
(Weeping) Ash	18.02. - 17.03	Nion / Ash Moon
Alder	18.03. - 14.04.	Fearn / Alder Moon
Willow	15.04. - 17.05.	Saille / Willow Moon
Hawthorn	18.05. - 09.06.	Uath / Hawthorn Moon
Oak	10.06. - 07.07.	Duir / Oak Moon
Holly	08.07. - 04.08.	Tinne / Holly Moon
Hazel bush	05.08. - 01.09.	Coll / Hazel Moon
Vine	02.09. - 29.09	Muin / Vine Moon
Ivy	30.09. - 27.10.	Gort / Ivy Moon
Reed	28.10. - 24.11.	Negetal / Reed Moon
Elderberry	25.11. - 22.12.	Ruish / Elder Moon
The day between the years	23.12.	

Four main trees mark change of seasons

The basis of the Celtic tree circle is the "Celtic cross", which divides the year into its four seasons. Spring, summer, autumn and winter are ushered in by the winter solstice in December and the summer solstice in June, as well as the equinoxes in March and September.

Four main trees mark the beginning of each season:
Oak ~ Spring / Birch ~ Summer / Olive tree ~ Autumn / Beech ~ Winter

On these days the Celts celebrated their important sun festivals:
Ostara: Spring equinox (20.03.)
Litha: Summer solstice (21.06.)
Mabon: Equinox in autumn (23.09.)
Yule: Winter Solstice (21.12.)

On the so-called cross-quarter days, dated exactly between the solstices and the equinoxes, they celebrated their lunar festivals:
Imbolc (02.02.), **Beltane** (01.05.), **Lughnasadh / Lammas** (23.09.) and **Samhain** (01.11.).

Sagittarius 23.11. – 21.12.

People born under the sign of Sagittarius are usually mentally lively, enthusiastic, energetic, optimistic, athletic and open-minded. However, they can also be restless, too impulsive and reckless.

> Good time for magic work, the business affairs,
> Travel, publications and
> Truth / sincerity has as its object

Planet: Zeus (Jupiter) / **Angel:** Sachiel / **Olympian spirit:** Bethor / **Element:** fire / **Lucky stones:** brilliant, lapis lazuli, turquoise, sapphire / **Colors:** red, purple, yellow, green, royal blue / **Lucky day:** Thursday / **Lucky Numbers:** 4, 14, 24 / **Flowers:** carnation, daisy, iris / **Metal:** pewter / **Animals:** horse, deer, peacock, swan, elephant / **Body parts influenced:** Hips, thighs, liver, veins

Sagittarius in 2024

2024 will bring great opportunities into your life that will show you in a very good light and help you finally move forward with your long-cherished plans. You can and should be proud of what you have already achieved. The past few years have been very turbulent for you, but you are not giving up. On the contrary, this gave you the necessary drive to courageously initiate necessary changes, especially in your job and in your everyday life. You will fully implement these in 2024. Uranus brings you in contact with a new reality and changed conditions, especially in the professional field. You will have to take on more responsibility and additional tasks. The whole planetary picture of this year shows that the continuation of your path will once again become quite adventurous. All your efforts will be successful, even if you will get many a stone in the way from your colleagues at work. In return, your family will support you in all your decisions, treat you with much love and thus give you strength and optimism. In short, the "family-work" axis will play an important role for you this year and next. Trust in your abilities. In 2024, many things will change for the better. You will face some challenges, but you will be able to deal with and overcome them. On a financial level, you will go through profitable times and have the opportunity to make important investments.

Due to the many changes at work and in everyday life, your love life has been somewhat neglected in recent months, perhaps even years. Since things will still be quite turbulent at least in the first half of 2024, you will not really find time and peace to devote yourself to your love life again until summer. Use the calmer time now to fill your partnership with new sparkling life. And for the singles among those born under the zodiac sign Sagittarius, who have the desire for a relationship, it means: Open your heart for love and make room in your life for the person who is waiting for you in 2024 and will have a great influence on your future life.

Sagittarius: love, family and friends

Don't get too carried away with your initial successes and become so consumed with your career that your love life falls by the wayside. Don't overestimate your strengths and, despite all your work and enthusiasm for the innovations in life, also make room for your partnership.

Only if you manage to bring all areas of your life into harmony will you find the perfect happiness you have been working towards for so long. Consciously take time for your partner, show your love and appreciation, listen and do not exclude him/her from your "new" life. The same applies in principle to the singles among the Sagittarians who are looking for a partner: If you have the desire for a relationship, then you must also take the necessary time for it and show initiative, for example, go to places where you can possibly find a suitable partner. Because the chances are very good in 2024 that you will meet your dream person who will significantly influence your future life. 2024 will help you to fulfill many of your romantic dreams!

After a time full of misunderstandings and quarrels, peace, happiness and harmonious togetherness will finally return to your family life in 2024. To keep it that way permanently, let your family share your feelings and professional experiences.

In 2024, give not only your professional life a new direction, but also your social environment. Make new acquaintances and through this also get to know new areas in which you can get involved. Don't be afraid to make a difference in the lives of those around you, too, by openly addressing injustices and things you disagree with. Support those who cannot help themselves in a particular situation. You will be greatly thanked for this.

Sagittarius: profession and finances

From January to April you will face some challenges that will hinder your professional progress. After that, things will calm down and you can get back to focusing on your work and building your career. Proceed with strategy and plan. Get help and help others. This is how you build professional partnerships that benefit everyone. You have leadership qualities and can do a lot by motivating your employees if you really believe in yourself.

Financial abundance awaits you in 2024, but since unexpected expenses may arise in the middle of the year, it's important to be well prepared for them and mindful when spending money. It is quite possible that you will have to spend some money on the health of your loved ones. It is also important that you settle your debts as soon as possible, if you have any. You have worked hard and now have the financial potential to create a solid foundation for your future through smart investments. However, wait with monetary transactions until mid-May and generally do not make any risky monetary transactions. Rather build on security, even if the profits are a bit lower.

Sagittarius: health

If there's one thing that will really take a big hit in 2024, it's your overall well-being. It suffers from the pressure of your professional career and it is very important that you create gaps in your busy schedule to rest and do good to your mind and body.

November / December

CW 48	♐	**Sagittarius** 23.11. – 21.12.
Mon 25 -	☾ ☽	International Day for the Elimination of Violence against Women, St. Katharina
Tue 26	♂ ☽	
Wed 27	☿ ☽	Rise of Baha'u'llah - Baha'i
Thu 28	♃ ☽	Thanksgiving
Fri 29	♀ ☽	
Sat 30 +	♄ ☽	St. Andrew's Day
Sun 1	☉ ○	**new moon**, First Advent Sunday, St. Eligius

Monthly trend December	love	friends, family	profession, money
Aries	☼☼☼☼	☼☼☼☼☼	☼☼☼☼☼
Taurus	☼☼☼☼	☼☼☼☼	☼☼☼☼
Gemini	☼☼	☼☼☼☼☼	☼☼☼☼☼
Cancer	☼☼☼☼☼☼	☼☼☼☼	☼☼
Leo	☼☼☼☼☼	☼☼☼☼☼	☼☼☼☼☼
Virgo	☼☼☼☼	☼☼☼	☼☼☼☼☼
Libra	☼☼☼☼	☼☼☼☼☼	☼☼☼☼
Scorpio	☼☼☼☼☼	☼☼☼☼☼	☼☼☼☼☼
Sagittarius	☼☼☼☼☼	☼☼☼☼	☼☼☼☼
Capricorn	☼☼	☼☼☼☼☼	☼☼☼☼
Aquarius	☼☼☼☼☼	☼☼	☼☼☼☼☼
Pisces	☼☼☼☼☼	☼☼☼☼☼	☼

Ares and what suits him

Day: Tuesday / **Angels: Samael**, Satael, Amaviel / **Olympian spirit**: Phaleg / **Organs:** bile, blood, oxygen supply, muscles, teeth / **Mental aspects:** conflict ability, assertiveness, self-confidence / **Chakras:** throat and solar plexus / **Zodiac signs**: Aries and Scorpio / **Colors:** red, copper / **Metals:** iron, copper / **Animals:** wolf, cat, hawk, raven, tiger, horse / **Woods, trees**: cedar, oak / **Plants, herbs:** wormwood, acanthus, black belladonna, wild artichoke, white germer / **Incense, oils:** spurge (euphorbia), bdellium resin, hellebore (veratrum album), rhubarb, radish, iron dust / **healing stones:** ruby, jasper, antimony, sulfur

The Hours of Ares are suitable for discussions, contests, incantations and rituals involving hatred and enmity. They are especially suitable for summoning souls from the underworld or from soldiers killed in war.

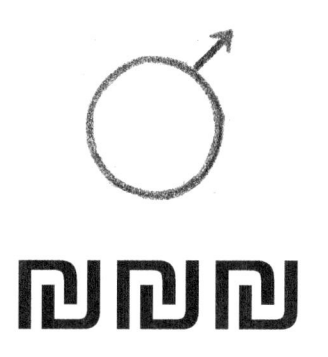

December

CW 49	♐	**Sagittarius** 23.11. – 21.12.
		🌾 **Hornbeam - Tree of perseverance:** *02. - 11.12.*
Mon 2	☾)	† *Saint Porphyrios, the Kapsokalyvite,* St. Bibiana, International Day for the Abolition of Slavery
Tue 3	♂)	International Day of People with Disabilities
Wed 4	☿)	† *Barbara, the Great Martyr*
Thu 5	♃)	
Fri 6	♀)	St. Nicholas Day
Sat 7	♄)	💎 *Shalako Dances (Zuni Pueblo),* St. Ambrosius
Sun 8	☉ ◐	**half moon waxing**, Second Advent Sunday "Prepare the way of the Lord", Feast of the conception of the Virgin Mary

~ 138 ~

December

KW 50	♐	**Sagittarius** *23.11. – 21.12.*
		🌿 **Fig tree – Tree of unison:** *12. - 21.12.*
Mon 9	☾ ●	✝ *Feast of the Conception by St. Anne of the Most Holy Theotokos*
Tue 10 +	♂ ●	Human Rights Day
Wed 11	☿ ●	
Thu 12	♃ ●	💎 *Our Lady of Guadalupe Feast Day (Pojoaque Pueblo)*
Fri 13	♀ ●	Lucia Day
Sat 14	♄ ●	
Sun 15 -	☉ ○	**full moon: Cold Moon**, Third Advent Sunday "Gaudete, be happy!"

~ 139 ~

December Full moon
Cold Moon

The beginning of winter around 21 December brings bitter cold
to the homeland of the Native American Indigenous.
That is why they call the full moon in December "Cold Moon".

Properly cleanse and consecrate ritual objects

Please be sure to energetically cleanse all bought materials and tools before use! All spiritual tools should be incensed with the appropriate incense for the magical process; also the candle you need for your ritual. Normally, you should make your own magical tools. It is very important that you use your spiritual tools exclusively for your magical work and in no case for other purposes, such as domestic use. Ideally, you should spiritually cleanse your ritual tools with holy water before their first use and then at regular intervals on the day of Hermes (Wednesday) and in one of its planetary hours on that day. To do this, dip in the holy water with a bundle of herbs consisting of rosemary, marjoram and mint, and then sprinkle it on your magical implements. Say while doing this:

Holy water, source of life,
Please sanctify my _____ .
Free it from negative energies and
protect it from the grip of evil creatures.
Let it be as pure as the snow on the High Mountains.
Amin.

Ritual magic mirror

For witches and sorcerers who practice mirror magic, a magic mirror is essential. In mirror magic, the mirror is a symbol of the transience of life and the "Otherworld". Therefore, mirror magic is associated with the realm of the dead or the summoning of the dead. The mirror is here to be understood as a kind of gateway into the "Mirror World" of the dead. But with the magic mirror witches and sorcerers can also "catch" negative energies and send them back (reflection of the mirror).

December

CW 51	♑	**Capricorn** *22.12. - 19.01.* (previously Sagittarius)
Mon 16	☾ ●	
Tue 17	♂ ●	St. Lazarus
Wed 18	☿ ●	
Thu 19	♃ ●	
Fri 20 +	♀ ●	International Day of Human Solidarity
Sat 21	♄ ●	**Yule**, winter solstice, beginning of winter, St. Thomas' Night
Sun 22	☉ ◐	**half moon waning,** Fourth Advent Sunday, **Capricorn > 19.01.** † *Royal hour of Jesus Christ's birth*

Yule 21. *December*

Yule is probably the most important annual festival, the day when the goddess gives birth to God. It is Christmas, even though in Christianity Christmas, which is the most important celebration along with Easter, takes place a few days later. Both Christian festivals are influenced by the ancient religion. **On Yule is winter solstice (sun is 0 degrees in Capricorn)** and now days are getting longer again. When God Sun is born, people celebrate the light that is so missing in winter months. That is why many light bringing candles shine in the house. We also celebrate the abundance, fertility and richness of goods on the day of God's birth. The most famous and probably the best known way to celebrate abundance was and is the Christmas tree decorated with candles and apples, lemons, oranges, pears and other winter fruits and berries.

Red, green and gold are the colors for the Yul festival. As altar decorations are suitable evergreen branches, for example, from the spruce, fir or holly. Incense mixtures of myrrh, frankincense, myrtle and mistletoe are suitable.

Cronos and what suits him

Day: Saturday / **Angels**: Cassiel (Kaviel), Machatan, Uriel / **Olympian spirit**: Aratron / **Organs**: spleen , skeleton / **Mental aspects**: Psychic stability, overcoming fears / **Chakra**: Root / **Zodiac signs**: Capricorn and Aquarius / **Color**: green / **Metal**: lead / **Animals**: cat, billy goat, owl, bat, eel, starfish / **Woods, trees**: cork oak, beech, fir, cypress, cedar / **Plants, herbs**: monkshood, asphodelus, cactus, hemlock, coca bush, fennel, black henbane, mandragora, poppy / **Incense, oils**: black poppy seed, black henbane, mandragora root, myrrh, magnetic iron dust / **Healing stones**: turquoise, chalcedony, obsidian, fossil with calamite inclusion

The hours of Cronos are ideal for inner contemplation, seclusion, and thoughtful actions. They are a good time for incantations and rituals involving hatred and enmity.

December

CW 52	♑	**Capricorn** 22.12. – 19.01.
		🌿 *Apple Tree - Tree of love: 23.12. – 01.01.*
Mon 23	☾	
Tue 24	♂	Christmas Eve, † *Διονύσια* † ✝ *Great Liturgy of the Nativity of Christ,* 💠 *Christmas Eve (Acoma and Nambe Pueblo)*
Wed 25	☿	**1st Christmas Day** (birth of Jesus Christ) 💠 *is also celebrated by most Pueblo,* beginning of the "Rauh" Nights (until 06.01), **Birthday of Sun God Mithras,** J *Hanukkah (until 02.01.2025)*
Thu 26 -	♃	**2nd Christmas Day,** St. Stephen's Day, ✝ *Synaxis of the Most Holy Mother of God*
Fri 27	♀	St. Johannes
Sat 28	♄	Day of the innocent children (14.000 children – holy innocents – slain by Herod in Bethlehem) 💠 *is also celebrated by the Picuris Pueblo*
Sun 29 +	☉	

Sun god Mithras

On 25. December the birthday of the Sun god Mithras is celebrated. What is celebrated today by Christians as the birth of Jesus has much older tradition. Christmas existed before Christianity and was adopted by it only in the 4th century AD. Before that, other cultures celebrated Christmas as a festival of the winter solstice. A new religion, the cult of Mithras, arose in Rome around the year 70 before our time. It believed in the immortality of the soul, in resurrection, and also in the doctrine of the Trinity. Mithras was seen as the savior and redeemer who would return to judge the living and the dead.

Our Aura: Visible energy of the soul

The human aura is a very sensitive and dynamic, and therefore changeable, force that reflects one's strengths and fragilities. It is in constant change within a fixed basic structure and countless internal and external factors constantly interact with it. It is an expression of the life force that energizes the whole being - mentally, physically and spiritually. It has the ability to adapt and renew itself. A healthy, strong aura can spontaneously bind positive influences, meaning it can be used to reject negative influences. Depending on the influences, it can come to a contamination and therefore weakening of this wonderful, power-giving protective shield. This can have many causes. Biological, environmental, emotional and social factors and even conditions and future happenings unknown to ourselves can have an enormous influence on the aura. Negative thinking, feeling and acting, unhealthy diet, environmental pollution, traumatic experiences, stress, karmic entanglements, influence of spiritual entities or even manipulative attacks, curses by hostile witches or sorcerers ... All this can weaken the aura, make it porous. Many people are even born with a dirty aura, caused by the sins of their forefathers.

Why is it important to cleanse your aura?

The more you wear a shirt, the dirtier it becomes and then it has to be washed. The same applies to the aura, which must be spiritually "washed", meaning cleaned, again and again. It is very important to keep one's aura clean and thereby strong. People with a weakened aura feel permanently burdened, lacking energy, strength and protection. Many illnesses, which are later expressed on a physical level, show up beforehand in the aura. Therefore, purifying the aura can eliminate illnesses in the beginning and actually treat them causally.

$$\Omega \diamondsuit \Omega$$

If you want to multiply, you have to share.

Pythagoras

December

CW 1	♑	*Capricorn* 22.12. – 19.01.
Mon 30	☾	
	☽	
Tue 31	♂ ○	New Year's Eve
	☽	

The magic of the "Rauh" Nights

The "Rauh" Nights are the 12 special nights between Christmas and Epiphany (25.12. to 06.01.). In the past, they were considered a good time to summon or exorcise spirits, to communicate with animals or to tell fortunes. The "Rauh" Nights are a time to pause, reflect on the past, put things in order and let go of what is disturbing. They are a time to consider what the future should look like, what we want to have in our lives and what we don't. Around this dark time with only short daylight phases are entwined divinations, customs and rituals, some of which are many centuries old.

The exact origin of the "Rauh" Nights is not clear to this day. Possibly it goes back to the Germanic lunar calendar. According to this, a year has twelve lunar months with a total of 354 days. **The eleven days or twelve nights missing to the today's solar calendar were considered as days outside of the time.** Therefore, probably also the expression "between the years", with which exactly this time between Christmas and the Epiphany is meant. Another important reason was certainly that the Christmas season has always been a time off from work. People came together, celebrated, and told each other stories, and also stories of eerie encounters in the dark. People believed that **during the "Rauh" Nights many spirits** were on the move. **Percht is the goddess of the "Rauh" Nights, who is supposed to watch over the fact that people do not work and come to rest. This folk belief is especially widespread in the Alpine country.** There Percht is depicted as a hooded fur figure with a mask and bells.

The origin of the word "Rauh" Nights is also not clear. A connection to "furry" or "hairy" in allusion to the alpine Perchten figure is possible. Also the reference to the fumigation of the houses with incense, which was practiced for the protection against evil spirits in the Christmas season, is conceivable.

The "Rauh" Nights were and are signposts for what is coming and an important time for divination and oracles. That is why the **pouring of lead on New Year's Eve** is still a popular custom today. **Also the incense is an old ritual for the time of the "Rauh" Nights.** Old, negative energies are incensed out with it, in order to start unencumbered into the new year. **Very suitable for this is an incense with star anise, cardamom, cinnamon bark, lavender, frankincense, spruce resin, pine needles and salt. The "Rauh" Nights are also very good for manifesting wishes.** Therefore, it is important to devote ourselves to our inner being, our thoughts and feelings during this time, because they have an influence on the outer world.

"Rauh" Night Ritual, to manifest a wish

What you need:

- 1 small blue candle
- 1 small sheet of paper
- 1 bay leaf
- 1 pen
- 1 tweezers
- Incense that goes with Zeus (aloe wood, storax resin, gum resin) or especially for the time of the "Rauh" Nights (see above)
- Matches or lighter
- 1 Vessel for incense
- 1 small box (an empty matchbox for example)

Choose the **planetary time of Zeus** for the ritual and if possible perform this ritual on one of the two Thursdays in the time of the "Rauh" Nights. Thursday is the day of Zeus. Prepare all the utensils listed above and place ready in the place you have chosen for your ritual. Come to rest and carefully make the laurel leaf burn with a match or lighter. Then use it to light your candle and the incense.

Push all disturbing thoughts aside and concentrate on your wish that you want to manifest. Formulate it precisely and clearly and write it down on the small piece of paper with a pen. Imagine how everything should be – as if it had already happened. The more detailed you can do this, the better.

Then fold the leaf, so many times until it can not be folded smaller. With the tweezers, hold the folded leaf in the incense and then over the candle flame. Let it burn completely until only ash remains. Pour this into the small box. Take it in both hands while speaking in a clear, firm voice:

Zeus, you mighty and benevolent ruler,
Zeus, you light and hearty magnate.
Allow me my wish.
Zeus, gracious lord, ruler of Olympus,
light of the world: Please help me to reach my goal.

Keep the candle burning until it goes out by itself. Then bury the box with the ashes in your favorite place of power in the garden or outdoors and try to mentally let go of your wish.

Artavan, the unknown fourth Holy King

A tradition says that besides the known three Holy Kings, there was a fourth Holy King. But he failed to reach the birthplace of the Savior at the right time and spent his whole life searching for the living God, Jesus Christ. His name was Artavan, he came from Persia and he was a friend of the other three Holy Kings, Melchior, Caspar and Balthazar, who worshipped Jesus Christ shortly after his birth in the stable of Bethlehem. And he was a magician and astronomer who had also seen the conjunction of the planets indicating the point of birth of a king. So he went to his friends who lived in Babylon. Then they would travel together to the place where the bright star would shine, there where the birth of the new king would take place. On the way, however, he came across a fevered Hebrew in the desert, whom he cared for. Because of his help, however, he was delayed, and when he finally arrived at the appointed meeting place, the Three Holy Kings had already departed. He tried to catch up with them, but he did not succeed and finally arrived in Bethlehem at the time when Herodes had the countless babies killed for fear of competition. Artavan intervened and bribed a soldier with a ruby that he wanted to bring as a gift to the Divine Child to release a child. This child was John the Forerunner.

Artavan then went to Egypt and stayed there for 33 years, doing much of good: healing sick people without asking money for it, freeing innocent prisoners by paying their convictions, and associating with the helpless and humble. When he finally returned to Jerusalem, it happened to be the day of Jesus Christ's crucifixion.

At the moment he asked about the crucified King of the Jews, the great earthquake occurred at Solomon's Temple, which was destroyed by a huge crack. A large stone fell on Arvantan's head and he slumped down unconscious. When he came to his senses after some time, he said: "33 years I have searched for you, but never seen you face to face or served you, my King." Then he heard a sweet voice saying to him: "Amen, Amen. I tell you, whatever you did to one of these poor brothers of mine, you did to me." Then Artavan opened his eyes and saw Jesus Christ for a short moment in a brilliantly bright light. Blessed to have met the Savior after all, Artavan died in deep peace.

The relics of the Three Holy Kings are said to have been brought to Constantinople by Empress Helena, mother of the Byzantine Emperor Constantine. From there, they arrived in Milan after the plundering of Constantinople ordered by the Vatican. This plundering was undertaken by mercenary crusaders hired by the richest Milanese family (the oldest palace in the center of Milan, now converted into a hotel, is incidentally owned by this family). After the conquest of the city by Emperor Friedrich I (reigned 1152 - 1190), the Imperial Chancellor and the Archbishop of Cologne, Rainald von Dassel, transported the relics then to the Cologne Cathedral, where they arrived in July 1164. The bones of Artavan were taken to France.

Icon of the Blessed Virgin Mary with the child Jesus in her arms - well protected in the Holy Mount Athos in northern Greece. Mary's facial expression is full of infinite mercy, love, compassion and motherly tenderness. Although Jesus Christ is depicted as an infant, he has a serious face because he is a judge.

At the beginning of the 14th century, on 21. January, the monks in a monastery in the Holy Mountain retreated to their cells to rest until their daily care began. Very early then, the main gate of the monastery would be opened. The monks did not know that pirates were waiting outside, having surrounded the monastery, ready to invade to plunder everything. The abbot was alone in the church, devoting himself to his prayer. He suddenly flinched when he heard a voice that did not sound like a human voice. Frightened, he looked around. But nobody was there. And yet someone was speaking, he hears it quite clearly. He concentrated and now became aware that the icon of the Virgin Mary was speaking to him, and he listened in full of awe. She said: "Do not open the gate of the monastery today, but chase away the pirates after you have climbed the walls."

Surprised, the abbot looked at the portrait of the Virgin Mary and could hardly believe what he was seeing: the shape of her was alive. The same goes for the Child Jesus, whom she held in her arms. He moved his right hand and placed it over the mouth of his holy mother, while he turned his radiant face toward her. A sweet child's voice was heard saying: "No Mother, don't tell them. Let them be punished for failing in their solitary duties, as they deserve." Then the Blessed Mother, with great motherly care for her only son, raised her hand slightly, held his small hand, bent her holy face a little to the right, and repeated more insistently: "Do not open the gate of the monastery today. After you have climbed the walls, drive out the pirates. And pay penance, because my son is justly angry with you." After repeating the warning for the third time, life faded from the icon again.

An interactive matrix or just an old fairy tale? In any case, this icon still exists today well protected in the Holy Mountain of Athos in northern Greece. But in fact, its present appearance is different from the one before it came to life to warn the monks of the planned attack. In its present form, it is not human-made, but was created by the grace of God after the miraculous intervention of the Holy Mother Mary to save the monastery. In this sense, the monks of the monastery and believers around the world venerate this icon, which is also called "Panagia Paramythia".

The icon is said to have many miracles. The legend says that Jesus was so strict because the monks at that time had accumulated a lot of wealth in the monastery instead of giving it to the poor. The monks had not done their duties with humility as they should have. After the miraculous rescue, they gave all the wealth to the poor and worked twice as hard as before to do penance and thank Mother Mary and Jesus Christ for their help. For centuries, in front of the icon burns an olive oil light, whose flame never goes out. This is made sure for generations by the monks of Mount Athos.

☾ Moon Calendar 2024 ☽

	01	02	03	04	05	06	07	08	09	10	11	12
1	●	●	●	●	☾ +	☾	☾	☾	(	(	○ +	○
2	●	● -	●	☾	☾ +	☾	☾ +	☾ -	(	○	)	)
3	● +	☾	☾ +	☾	☾	☾ +	☾	(	○	) -	)	)
4	☾	☾	☾	☾	☾ +	☾ -	☾	○	) -	)	)	)
5	☾	☾	☾	☾ +	☾	☾ +	☾ -	) +	)	)	)	)
6	☾	☾	☾	☾	☾ +	○	○ +	) +	) +	)	) -	)
7	☾	☾ +	☾	☾	☾	) +	)	) +	)	)	)	)
8	☾	☾ +	☾	○	○	)	)	)	)	)	)	☽
9	☾	○	☾ +	)	) +	) +	)	)	)	) -	☽	☽
10	☾ +	) -	○	)	) -	)	) +	) +	) +	☽	☽	☽ +
11	○	)	)	)	)	)	)	)	☽ -	☽	☽	☽
12	) -	)	) +	)	)	)	)	☽	☽	☽	☽	☽
13	)	)	) -	)	)	) +	) +	☽ -	☽ +	☽ +	☽ +	☽
14	)	)	) +	)	) +	☽	☽	☽ +	☽	☽	☽	☽
15	)	)	)	☽	☽	☽	☽	☽ +	☽	☽	●	● -
16	)	☽	) +	☽	☽	☽	☽	☽	☽ +	●	●	●
17	)	☽ -	☽	☽ +	☽ -	☽	☽	☽	●	●	●	●
18	☽	☽ +	☽	☽ -	☽	☽	☽ +	☽	● +	●	●	●
19	☽	☽	☽ -	☽	☽	☽ -	●	●	●	●	●	●
20	☽	☽	☽	☽ -	☽ -	☽ -	●	●	●	●	●	● +
21	☽	☽	☽	☽	☽	●	●	●	●	● +	●	●
22	●	● -	●	●	●	●	●	●	●	●	(	●
23	● -	●	● -	●	● +	●	●	●	●	●	(+	(
24	●	●	●	●	●	●	●	●	●	●	(	(
25	○	●	○	●	●	●	●	●	(+	(-	(
26	●	●	●	●	●	●	●	●	(	(	(	(-
27	● +	●	●	●	●	●	(-	(-	(-	(	(
28	●	●	● -	●	●	☾	☾	(	(	(	(
29	●	●	●	● -	(	(	(	(	(	(	(+
30	●		●	● -	☾	☾ +	☾	(+	(	(+	○
31	● +		●		(		(	(-		(+		)

○ Full Moon   ○ New Moon
☽ Half Moon waxing (first quarter)   ☾ Half Moon waning (last quarter)

) Waxing Moon   ● Waxing Moon domed   ☾ Waning Moon
● Waning Moon domed   + spiritually positive day   - spiritually negative day

~ 151 ~

✡ Witch Festivals ✡ Moons ✡ Eclipses ✡ Zodiac Signs

01	CAPRICORN 22.12.-19.01.	01.01. Goddess Nanshe / 04.01. ◐ / 11.01. ○ / 18.01. ◑ / 25.01. ● Wolf Moon
02	AQUARIUS 20.01.-18.02.	01.02 Goddess Juno Februata / 02.02. IMBOLC ~ midwinter / 03.02. ◐ / 16.02. Goddess Hecate / 09.02. ○ / 16.02. ◑ / 24.02. ● Snow Moon
03	PISCES 19.02.-20.03.	03.03. ◐ / 20.03. OSTARA ~ equinox, beginning of spring / 10.03. ○ / 17.03. ◑ / 24./25.03. lunar eclipse / 25.03. ● Worm Moon
04	ARIES 21.03.-20.04.	02.04. ◐ / 08.04. ○ ~ solar eclipse / 15.04. ◑ / 24.04. ● Pink Moon / 30.04. Walpurgis Night
05	TAURUS 21.04.-20.05.	01.05. BELTANE ~ midspring / 23.05. ● Flower Moon / 01.05. ◐ / 18.05. God Panas / 08.05. ○ / 15.05. ◑
06	GEMINI 21.05.-21.06.	01.06. Goddess Carna / 06.06. ○ / 09.06. Goddess Estia / 14.06. ◑ / 21.06. LITHA ~ summer solstice, beginning of summer / 22.06. ● Strawberry Moon / 28.06. ◐
07	CANCER 22.06.-22.07.	06.07. ○ / 14.07. ◑ / 21.07. ● Buck Moon ~ Goddess Cerridwen / 28.07. ◐
08	LEO 23.07.-23.08.	01.08. LUGNASADH ~ midsummer / 04.08. ○ / 12.08. ◑ / 19.08. ● Sturgeon Moon / 26.08. ◐
09	VIRGO 24.08.-22.09.	03.09. ○ / 11.09. ◑ / 13.09. Goddess Aphrodite / 17./18.09. lunar eclipse / 18.09. ● Corn Moon / 23.09. MABON ~ equinox, beginning of autumn / 24.09. ◐
10	LIBRA 23.09.-22.10.	02.10. ○ ~ solar eclipse / 10.10. ◑ / 11.10. Goddess Demeter / 17.10. ● Hunter's Moon ~ lunar eclipse / 24.10. ◐ / 31.10. Halloween
11	SCORPIO 23.10.-22.11.	01.11. ○ ~ SAMHAIN ~ mid autumn / 09.11. ◑ / 15.11. ● Beaver Moon / 23.11. ◐
12	SAGITTARIUS 23.11.-21.12.	01.12. ○ / 08.12. ◑ / 15.12. ● Cold Moon / 21.12. YULE ~ winter solstice, beginning of winter / 22.12. ◐ / 25.12. Mithras, God of the Sun ~ beginning of „Rauh" Nights (until 06.01.)

● full moon   ○ new moon   ◐ half moon waning   ◑ half moon waxing

Spiritually positive and negative days

January: +3, +10, +27, +31, -12, -23 / February: +7, +8, +18, -2, -10, -17, -22 / March: +3, +9, +12, +14, +16, -13, -19, -23, -28 / April: +5, +17, -18, -20, -29, -30 / May: +1, +2, +4, +6, +9, +14, -10, -17, -20 / June: +3, +5, +7+9, +13, +23, -4, -20 / July: +2, +6, +10, +13, +18, +30, -5, -19, -27 / August: +5, +6, +7, +10, +14, +15, -2, -13, -27, -31 / September: +6, +10, +13, +18, +30, -4, -11, -27 / October: +13, +16, +21, +25, +31, -3, -9, -27 / November: +1, +13, +23, +30, -6, -25 / December: +10, +20, +29, -15, -26

Magic processes and planets

You can use the characteristics of a planet for your magical work. Give it more spiritual power by choosing the right planets, days and hours. Here you can see what processes each planet supports:

Helios (Sun) – **Sunday:** growth, vitality, healing, creativity and will

Selene (Moon) – **Monday:** emotions, eroticism, subconscious, intuition, divination and memories of the past

Ares (Mars) – **Tuesday:** assertiveness, conflict ability, self-confidence, action, courage, physical abilities

Hermes (Mercury) – **Wednesday:** communication, connection between soul, mind and body

Zeus (Jupiter) – **Thursday:** growth, professionalism, abundance and wealth, success and health

Aphrodite (Venus) – **Friday:** love, sexuality, beauty, art, harmony and social relations

Cronos (Saturn) – **Saturday:** responsibility, discipline, psychological stability, overcoming fears, discarding bad habits and obsessions

The phases of the moon and the matching gardening

Waxing Moon: "Exhalation of the Earth"
In its filling phase, the moon attracts the plant sap and lets it flow into the upper parts of the plant. Above-ground growth therefore receives impulses during this time and it is the best time to work on plants that bear fruit.

- Sowing and planting leafy, fruiting and flowering plants
- Transplanting seedlings and grafting plants
- Grass reseeding
- Harvesting (for immediate fresh consumption only)

Full Moon
Full Moon means the changing of waxing and waning. When the moon is full, these two impulses are in balance and the power of the moon is strongest.

- Collecting medicinal herbs – their healing power is strongest then
- Fertilising – the ground absorbs nutrients particularly well
- No pruning of woody plants – injuries do more harm

Waning Moon: "Breathing in the earth"
When the moon is waning, the plants' forces retreat into the earth and underground growth is boosted during this phase.

- Harvesting, storage and preservation
- Pruning hedges / woody plants – plant juices are in the root zone
- Control of weeds and pests

New Moon
At new moon the moon is between earth and sun and does not reflect light. It is the time of "resting" and gathering strength for the new cycle.

- Work that serves the regeneration of plants – treatment of diseased plants or plants affected by pests

About the author

Nik W. D. Goodman is the "White Diamond", an internationally known esoteric master and a very powerful medium. He was born in Greece and is in spiritual contact with lightworkers all over the world. For many years he studied ancient scriptures and acquired a deep spiritual knowledge across all magical arts. Visions and contacts with other dimensions strengthened his conviction in the existence of an invisible world and a Higher Power that secretly guides us through our lives. Nik W. D. Goodman is in demand all over the world as a qualified parapsychologist, who with his charisma and his high spiritual abilities helps where special esoteric knowledge is needed.

Witchbook 2024

Publisher and responsible for the content:
Nik W. D. Goodman - The White Diamond

by Nik W. D. Goodman
This work including all contents is protected by copyright. All rights reserved. Reprinting or reproduction (even in part) in any form (print, photocopy or other process) as well as storage, processing, duplication and distribution using electronic systems of any kind, in whole or in part, is prohibited without the express written permission of the author. All translation rights reserved.

Disclaimer: *The use of this book and the implementation of the information contained therein is expressly at your own risk. The author accepts no liability on any legal grounds for any damage of any kind that may result from the practice of the rituals presented in this book. Legal claims and claims for damages are therefore excluded. The work, including all contents, has been compiled with the utmost care and the information contained therein has been compiled to the best of the author's knowledge and belief. The author assumes no liability for the topicality, correctness and completeness of the contents of the book, nor for printing errors. The author cannot accept any legal responsibility or liability in any form for incorrect information and any consequences arising therefrom.*

Nik W.D. Goodman

279 pages ~ to buy on AMAZON and EBAY, for example,
available in German, English and Greek language

Witchbook: The fundamental book of witchcraft Knowledge ★ Practice ★ Rituals

With this great Witchbook, Nik Goodman has created a unique fundamental book of witchcraft, which makes it easier for interested people to get started in the witchcraft art as well as for already experienced witches and sorcerers to use as a magical guide, reference book and inspiration for their magical work. This " Witch's Bible" summarises witchcraft knowledge gathered over several decades in a very comprehensive and well-structured way on more than 270 pages. Combined with the many powerful and detailed rituals described in the large practical chapter, this great basic book of witchcraft is an essential foundation and daily guide for every witch and sorcerer in their magical work. Excerpt from the contents:

Chapter 1: Witchcraft beliefs and rules
Basic principles and rules of witchcraft ★ The different sectors of witchcraft ★ Witches' Sabbaths and Cycle of the year ★ Admission to the coven and magical name

Chapter 2: Ritual objects, tools, aids and clothing
Equipping of a witch and how to consecrate it properly ★ What supports which magical process? ★ The ritual power of candles

Chapter 3: Witchcraft knowledge
Using the power of the moon ★ Magical processes and planets ★ Goddesses and Gods ★ Greek pantheon ★ Olympic spirits and their assignment to the planets ★ Archangels and Angels of the seasons ★ Signs of the zodiac and the 12 houses in astrology ★ Celtic tree horoscope ★ The ancient runes ★ Witchcraft alphabet: Theban ★ Spiritual meaning of numbers according to Pythagoras ★ Witch symbols: Pentagrams and more ★ Necromancy and Ouija ★ Divination arts

Chapter 4: Gems, herbs, ritual oils, amulets
The magic of gemstones ★ Magic plants and Mandragora ★ Make your own ritual oils, incense, powders and tinctures ★ The Magic of menstruation ★ Manogal Milk: one of the most powerful tools of magic ★ The power of amulets

Chapter 5: Rituals and prayers
Creating the magical circle: Invocation to the four cardinal points ★ Matrix Portal and Spiritus Locus ★ Ritual to catch and knot the wind ★ Witch broom ritual to get rid of unwanted guests ★ Egg Oracle ritual on Easter moon or Ostara ★ Ritual on Beltane to attract a person erotically ★ The 7 knot love ritual ★ Ritual for the flow of money ★ Dragon oil protection ritual ★ Ritual of the magic Selene's Full Moon Ring ★ Apple ritual on Mabon ★ Molybdomancy ritual on New Year's Eve to learn about the future partnership ★ Witch prayers

Magic
for Beginners

Grimoire
de Diamant Blanc

Nik W. D. Goodman

Magic for Beginners – Grimoire de Diamant Blanc

170 pages, to buy on AMAZON and EBAY, for example,
available in German, English, Spanish and French language

A comprehensive magical work that combines both theoretical and practical magical knowledge in a structured and generally understandable way. This book, illustrated throughout in color, opens a magical gateway even for those who have little experience with the magical arts, but want to engage with them with heart and mind.

Magic overview
~ What can you do with magic?
~ Magic arts and magic means

Magical depth
~ Wisdom and the power of magic
~ Basic principles for magical work

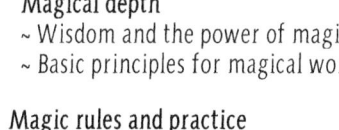

Magic rules and practice
~ Preparation of a magical ritual / tools and aids ~ Magic of gems ~ Planets, archangels and Olympian spirits with their symbols ~ Magical processes and planets ~ Using the power of the moon ~ Spiritually positive and negative days of each month ~ The signs of the zodiac, their characteristics and their counterparts ~ Witch festivals

Candles magic
Magic of candles, an almost forgotten art ~ Magic candle rituals: preparation, basics for practice ~ Shapes and colors: Which candles go with which rituals? ~ Increase the magical power of candles with engraving, oil and incense ~ The candle flame and what it shows us / The Almadel candle ~ Purifying the aura: What is the aura?

Candle rituals / prayers: to cleanse the aura ~ for lonely hearts ~ for happiness and harmony in the family and partnership ~ to win back a beloved person ~ to attract a person sexually ~ for the flow of money and professional and financial success ~ to render enemies harmless, to ward off slander and negative energy ~ for protection against astral attacks, dark powers, dark magic and curses ~ for inner peace and trust in the flow of life, God's guidance and the power of guardian angels ~ of the magical Selene full moon ring ~ for the welfare of humanity and peace in the world ~ for the harmony of all worlds and our connection to the universe

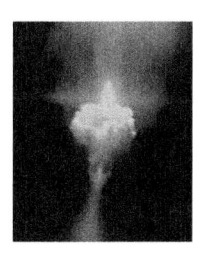

Magic is the art,
to make use of supernatural powers.
It is therefore the connection, becoming one with
the earthly natural elements, which in turn are
guided and strengthened by supersensible forces.
Nik W. D. Goodman

TASSEOGRAPHY
Coffee Ground and Tea Leaf Fortune Telling

LEXICON
700+ SYMBOLS

Nik W. D. Goodman

Magic for Beginners
Grimoire de Diamant Blanc 2

Tasseography – Coffee Ground and Tea Leaf Fortune Telling
including lexicon with over 700 symbols
134 pages, to buy on AMAZON and EBAY, for example,
available in German, English and Spanish language

Two very common methods of fortune telling are reading coffee grounds or tea leaves. Since time immemorial, people have been fascinated by the idea of making predictions and forecasts about the future. And tasseography is a relatively easy method to learn for this. This book explains very practically and clearly with many pictures and step by step how coffee grounds and tea leaves are interpreted and which rules apply.

~ What do you need to consider when reading?

~ Which position of the symbols gives you information about what?

~ What are the methods of interpretation?

~ How do you prepare yourself mentally?

~ How to properly prepare your mocha or tea for reading?

and much more

The very comprehensive dictionary of over 700 symbols makes this book a comprehensive primer on a fascinating segment of divination.

NEW in this 3rd revised edition: Tasseography rituals for love, for financial and professional success and for prophetic interpretation / Teas suitable for interpretation and their accompanying medicinal effects / Exciting background knowledge about coffee, its discovery and distribution and about the history of coffee guessing

44 pages,
to buy on AMAZON and EBAY, for example,
available in German, English and Greek language

„Coffee Ground Reading – simply explained" introduces the world of this popular method of fortune-telling in over 50 pages. In this compact book, the correct preparation of a mocha for coffee ground reading is explained and how it is interpreted. More than 350 symbols complete the book, which is ideal for starting the subject.

EGG ORACLE
Ovomancy, Oomancy, Ooscopy
Rituals and the secret of Egg Oracle
Lexicon 700+ Symbols

Nik W. D. Goodman

Magic for Beginners - Grimoire de Diamant Blanc 3

Egg Oracle – Ovomancy, Oomancy, Ooscopy
including lexicon with over 700 symbols

127 pages, to buy on AMAZON and EBAY, for example, available in German and English language

Ovomancy is a very ancient magical art. It knows countless variations and only very few people today really master this fantastic form of divination. This book initiates you into the secrets of the egg oracle and brings you the best-known and most promising method a very clear way: the interpretation of the egg white and egg yolk in the water glass.

Practical instructions help you with the preparation and realization and examples of pictures as well as a large lexicon with more than 700 symbols give you support in the interpretation.

The start of the egg oracle is made easier by powerful rituals, which are described in detail:

Ritual for a clear view into the future

Ritual for protection and divine assistance as well as harmony and love

Ritual for insights around pregnancy and birth

New Year's Eve ritual to learn about the future partnership

Ritual to help a worried person with wise advice

Protection ritual to recognize future dangers and obstacles

This book is the third book of our mystical book series after "Magic for Beginners – Grimoire de Diamant Blanc" and "Tasseography – Coffee Ground and Tea Leaf Fortune Telling".

CEROMANCY
METALOMANCY

Fire divination: wax and lead casting rituals
Lexicon 700+ Symbols

Magic for Beginners - Grimoire de Diamant Blanc 4

Nik W. D. Goodman

Ceromancy and Metalomancy
Fire divination: wax and lead casting rituals
including lexicon with over 700 symbols
160 pages, to buy on AMAZON and EBAY, for example,
available in German and English language

This remarkable book presents the ancient and almost forgotten oracular art of casting wax and lead, on which there is hardly any literature so far. Ceromancy and Molybdomancy are sectors of the ancient divination art of Pyromancy (Fire Oracle).
They know many methods of divination.

Some include the images of the candle flame used to melt the wax or metal in the interpretation. Others focus only on interpreting the cooled forms that emerge after casting into water. But each method makes use of fire. Practical descriptions help to prepare and carry out the method, and visual examples as well as a large lexicon with more than 700 symbols support the interpretation. The first steps into Ceromancy and Molybdomancy are made easier by powerful rituals, which are described in detail:

~ Yes-No rituals ~ Ritual for insights around pregnancy and birth ~ Ritual to learn about future financial situation and professional development ~ Ritual to see if you're a victim of black magic ~ Ritual to make black magic or the "evil eye" harmless ~ Ritual to find out, who or what is responsible for a suffering ~ Protection ritual to identify future dangers and obstacles ~ New Year's Eve ritual to learn about the future partnership ~ New Year's Eve ritual for the whole family

Lead Casting

Molybdomancy:
The Oracle Art of Metal Casting

350+
Symbols
for interpretation

Nik W. D. Goodman

69 pages, to buy on AMAZON and EBAY, for example, available in German, English and Greek language

Lead casting
Molybdomancy: The oracle art of metal casting
including rituals, interpretation examples and lexicon with over 350 symbols

Lead casting is a branch of the magical art of divination pyromancy (fire oracle), which dates back to ancient times. This book introduces the magical world of metal casting. The entry facilitates interpretation examples, a lexicon with over 350 symbols and powerful rituals:

~ Ritual to learn about future financial situation and professional development ~ Ritual to make black magic or the "evil eye" harmless ~ Protection ritual to identify future dangers and obstacles ~ New Year's Eve ritual to learn about future partnership ~ New Year's Eve ritual for the whole family

Printed in Great Britain
by Amazon